LEADING WIT

'. . . with Jesus leading the way . . .'
(Mk 10:32, NIV)

*

'God exalted him . . . as Leader . . .'
(Ac 5:31)

To
Ulrike, Michael and Simone
with
much gratitude

and to
Molemo Seutloali
with
special appreciation

About the author:

GÜNTER KRALLMANN, born in West Germany,
now lives in South Africa where he serves as a Bible teacher with
'Youth With A Mission'.

LEADING WITH JESUS

A Handbook
On Qualifications For Spiritual Leadership
For Individual And Group Study

Günter Krallmann

OM
publishing

Copyright © 1989 Günter Krallmann
Revised edition 1991
Printed by Jensco Ltd., Hong Kong

Published in 1998 by OM Publishing

04 03 02 01 00 99 98   7 6 5 4 3 2 1

OM Publishing is an imprint of Paternoster Publishing,
P.O. Box 300, Carlisle, Cumbria, CA3 0QS, U.K.
http://www.paternoster-publishing.com

The right of Günter Krallmann to be identified as the Author of this work has been
asserted by him in accordance with Copyright, Designs and Patents Act 1988.

British Library Cataloguing in Publication Data
A catalogue record for this book is available from the British Library.

ISBN 1-85078-329-2

All Bible references and quotations are based on the Revised Standard Version (1962),
unless otherwise indicated through the abbreviations – KJV: King James Version,
NAS: New American Standard Bible (1977), NIV: New International Version, New
York International Bible Society (1978, 1983).

Cover design by Mullin Design, Kendal
Typeset by WestKey Ltd, Falmouth, Cornwall
Printed in Great Britain by Clays Ltd., St Ives PLC

Contents

Preface

Years of experience in mission work have led me to the conviction that two major building-blocks for establishing the Church and for seeing the Great Commission fulfilled, are found in the twin concepts of discipleship and leadership training.

The handbook, FOLLOWING JESUS, addressed the first area by providing basic material on the understanding and practice of Biblical discipleship. Building on that foundation, LEADING WITH JESUS is set forth as a sequel, focusing on indispensable qualifications for effective spiritual leadership.

*

A worldwide leadership crisis has not only deeply affected politics, business, education and family life; it has also infiltrated church and mission work. A lack of vision, of strategy, efficiency and personnel on the one hand, as well as division and failure on the other, indicate the urgent need for both more and better leaders.

LEADING WITH JESUS attempts to help meet this need. It desires to assist those whom God called into positions of spiritual oversight (pastors, leaders of youth groups or home cells, missionaries, executives, administrators, etc.) in recognizing and unfolding their potential in God. At the same time it desires to offer them help in their efforts to promote the development and release of leadership capacities in those under their care.

In short, to see the purposes of God fulfilled and the future growth and expansion of His work secured, a chain reaction of proper leadership development comes to the fore as an absolutely crucial need of the hour – both out of strategic, pragmatic, as well as pastoral considerations.

*

Spiritual leadership as understood in the pages which follow is that kind of leadership in God's work which meets with divine approval and blessing, and thus contributes significantly to the building of His kingdom.

As a closer study of the Scriptures reveals, God is more interested in *who we are* before Him, than in *what we do* for Him. In other words, the Biblical view and concept of leadership is marked by a much stronger emphasis on character and attitudes than on task accomplishment.

Accordingly, LEADING WITH JESUS concentrates primarily on those qualities of Christian character which the Bible highlights as foundational for anyone who aspires towards spiritual leadership.

In the final analysis, it seems, all true spiritual leadership comes down to being and setting a godly example. Therefore, with the Lord Jesus having presented the perfect leadership prototype, the double perspective of modelling one's life according to His leadership pattern, and then communicating that Christ-like example to those desired to follow, has been made the guiding thought of the book.

*

Underlying the selection of the title, 'LEADING WITH JESUS,' is the fundamental insight that true Christian leadership, i.e. leading *for* Jesus, is only possible on the basis of leading *with* Jesus. That is, through Christian leadership to present Christ and to effectively direct His people, chiefly requires a close co-operative fellowship with Him. It means to be leading with Jesus as our overall leader (see 1 Pe 5:4), our leadership model (see Jn 13:15), our leadership mentor (see Mt 11:29), with His authority (see Lk 10:19), His enabling presence (see Jn 14:16–18), His strategy (see Mt 28:18–20), and His supporting intercession (see Heb 7:25).

To be effective in leading with Jesus necessitates neither educational degrees nor natural power of personality; rather, whoever is committed to a life of trustful obedience to the Lord Jesus, will find himself moulded increasingly into His leadership style.

*

In order to help the reader gain a deeper grasp of the Biblical requirements for genuine Christian leadership, the book essentially concentrates on communicating Scriptural truth. Particularly in a day and age where, even in Christian circles, there is a danger of being pre-occupied and captivated by clever management techniques, success formulas, etc., we do well to re-focus on the Biblical standard for the issues in question, and to heed Jesus' sobering statement that apart from Him we can't accomplish anything of relevance for the kingdom of God (see Jn 15:5). Moreover, a persistent Biblical orientation lends itself more than any other approach to communicating the timeless Scriptural truths in a way that is simple, practical and cross-culturally acceptable. With the utmost challenge in missions today to see indigenous leadership raised up, there is increased need for literature that seeks to avoid western ethnocentricity tending to impose an alien leadership style, and rather seeks to propose the Jesus style.

*

Intensive study of God's Word for the preparation of the manuscript opened my eyes to a fuller Scriptural view on essential qualifications – both of character and action – for efficient spiritual leadership. It is my heart's desire that, in various parts of the world, many whom God called to be leaders will be similarly enriched as they study the Biblical principles and examples presented in the book on hand. And while doing so, may they derive much insight, inspiration and encouragement, as well as experience the enabling assistance of the Holy Spirit as they seek to maximize their God-given potential in their pursuit of LEADING WITH JESUS.

Günter Krallmann
Lionelton, South Africa, October 1988

Acknowledgments

For the accomplishment of this publication, I feel heartily indebted to the obliging assistance of others. My special gratitude goes out:

- to my dear family for their prayerful support, consideration and sacrifice in facilitating many long hours of study
- to my wife Ulrike, in particular, for her kindness to patiently check the numerous Bible references
- to Shirley Bland for her valuable editorial advice
- to Kay Robinson for her amiable help in assuming the typing of the manuscript
- to Jensco Ltd for their much appreciated willingness to undertake the publishing of the material
- to God for granting me the vision, faith and strength for the realization of the project

How to Use this Handbook

A main motivation for writing this book has been the desire to let the Word of God speak for itself on key qualifications for spiritual leadership.

For this reason, a wealth of Biblical principles, references and examples has been offered. The approach of presenting the material in outline form was chosen in order to challenge and direct the reader to investigate the Scriptures on his own for further clarification and consolidation of truths communicated.

The material also lends itself very well to group study; accordingly, each chapter ends with a follow-up task.

For more extended study on the subject of spiritual leadership, the books quoted are warmly recommended.

It is hoped that once the precepts of this handbook have been personally acquired, the material will then be used as a tool for training others in effective leadership, thus complying with the Biblical expectation of both reproduction and multiplication.

. . . the method of training and producing Christian leaders is first to understand the method of Christ and then to put it into faithful and productive practice.
P.T. CHANDAPILLA (1)

It is a godly life-style that makes a spiritual leader what he ought to be so others can depend upon his leadership.
DAVID L. HOCKING (2)

True greatness, true leadership is achieved in selfless service to others.
TED W. ENGSTROM (3)

. . . leaders in the church have an obligation to set an example which will motivate others to godly living and faithful service.
CHUA WEE HIAN (4)

INTRODUCTION

1

Spiritual Leadership

'God exalted him . . . as Leader . . .'
(Ac 5:31)

A. WHY SPIRITUAL LEADERS ARE GREATLY NEEDED

- they take initiative for God   (see* Jdg 5:2, 2 Ch 14:2–4)
- they receive and communicate God's direction   (see Ex 25:22, Dt 5:5)
- they lead the way for God's people   (see Dt 10:11, 2 Ch 34:31–33)
- they motivate others to follow   (see Ne 2:17 + 18,1 Ch 12:16–18)
- they care for their followers   (see Heb 13:17, 1 Th 2:11)
- they take their followers' needs to God   (see Nu 27:5, 1 Sa 12:23)
- they facilitate their followers' progress   (see 1 Ki 11:28, 2 Co 13:9 + 10)
- they train their followers into leaders   (see Mk 1:17, 2 Ti 2:2)

B. NATURAL AND SPIRITUAL LEADERSHIP COMPARED

Natural:
- ambition
- self-reliance
- following human wisdom
- optimism
- desire to be served
- special privileges
- power of personality
- standard of success

Spiritual:
- humility
- dependence upon God
- seeking God's direction
- faith
- desire to serve
- special opportunities for service
- godliness
- standard of faithfulness

C. THE FAVOURITE BIBLICAL PICTURE FOR A SPIRITUAL LEADER: THE SHEPHERD

- God: Ge 49:24. Ps 23, 78:52, 80:1, 95:7, Isa 40:11, Eze 34:11–22
- Jesus: Mic 5:4, Jn 10:1–18 + 26–28, 1 Pe 2:25, Heb 13:20, Rev 7:17
- other Biblical leaders: 2 Sa 7:7, Ps 77:20, 78:70–72, Jn 21:15, Ac 20:28
    (Moreover, see Nu 27:17, Jer 3:15, 23:1–4, Eze 34:2–10, Zec 10:3)

---

* The term 'see' is used to indicate that the author refers to the implied rather than the obvious meaning of the Scripture in question.

D. GOD'S PROVISION FOR COPING WITH LEADERSHIP RESPONSIBILITY

– His call   (see 1 Co 1:26–28, Ro 11:29)   – His wisdom   (see Jas 1:5, 1 Co 1:30)
– His grace   (see 2 Co 3:5, 1 Co 15:10)   – His guidance   (see Jn 14:26, Jer 33:3)
– His power   (see Col 1:29, Php 4:13)   – His peace   (see 1 Co 14:33, Php 4:7)

E. SPIRITUAL LEADERSHIP ENDANGERED

– insecurities: e.g. fear, self-doubt, discouragement
– pressures: e.g. loneliness, busyness, tension of priorities, lack of finances
– temptations: e.g. pride, ambition, envy, greed, abuse of privileges
– attacks: e.g. criticism, accusations, rejection, satanic oppression

F. SAFEGUARDS FOR SPIRITUAL LEADERS

– love for Jesus   (see Jn 21:15–17)   – a clear conscience (see Ti 1:19, Ac 24:16)
– humility   (see Jas 4:6)   – God's anointing   (see 1 Jn 2:27 + 28)
– God's Word   (see Ps 119:105)   – prayer support   (see 2 Co 1:11, 1 Th 5:25)
– seeking God   – godly counsel
     (see 2 Ch 17:3–5; 12:14)   (Pr 11:14, see also Ex 18:17–24)

G. SPIRITUAL LEADERS ARE MADE RATHER THAN BORN

– potential leadership aptitude, in order to become properly developed, especially
   requires teachability, discipline and training (see Pr 12:24)
– even with a more limited leadership aptitude, one can – with the Holy Spirit's
   help – grow up to become an effective leader for God (see 1 Sa 2:7)

H. THREE PILLARS OF EFFECTIVE SPIRITUAL LEADERSHIP

– living a godly life   (see chapter 2)
– practising servanthood   (see chapter 3)
– setting an example for imitation   (see chapter 4)

For further consideration:
   Ponder over the variety of expressions used to describe different facets of the
   Lord Jesus' leadership (See e.g. Isa 9:6, Rev 1:5, 17:14, Ac 5:31, 1 Pe 5:4, Heb 6:20
   and 12:2)

2

The Godliness Principle

'... he who sees me sees him who sent me.'
(Jn 12:45)

A. EFFECTIVENESS IN LEADERSHIP DEPENDS ON GODLINESS IN THE LEADER

– Godliness gives credibility   (see Jos 1:16 + 17)
– Godliness exerts influence   (see Ge 39:21–23, 2 Ch 24:2)
– Godliness provides protection   (see 2 Pe 2:5)
– Godliness follows Jesus' example   (see Jn 14:9; 8:29)

B. THE ATTRACTIVENESS OF GODLINESS

– it evidences separateness unto God   (see Ps 4:3)
– it evidences the life Jesus' death enabled us to live   (see Tit 2:12–14, 2 Co 5:15)
– it evidences the 'family attributes' of
  God's children   (see Mal 2:15, Eph 5:1)
– it evidences God's transforming work in us   (see Php 2:13, Ro 12:1 + 2)
– it evidences the life-style most apt to bless others   (see 1 Pe 3:1, Ps 1:1–3)
– it evidences the life-style most fulfilling for ourselves   (see 1 Ti 4:8)
– it evidences the life-style preparing us for eternity   (see 1 Ti 4:8, Mt 22:11 + 12)

C. GREAT INCENTIVES FOR GODLINESS

– the desire to increasingly please God   (see 1 Th 4:1; Mt 3:17, Heb 11:5)
– the desire to increasingly grow into His likeness   (see Mt 5:48, Col 3:10)
– the desire to increasingly reflect His likeness   (see Mt 5:16, Lk 6:36)

D. GODLINESS IN CORRELATION

– with fear of God   (see Job 1:8, Ps 112)
– with holiness   (see 2 Pe 3:11, 2 Co 1:12)
– with righteousness   (see Lk 1:75, 1 Co 1:30)
– with blamelessness   (see Lk 1:6, Php 2:15)
– with Christ-likeness   (see 2 Co 4:4, Heb 1:3)

E. DIVINE RESOURCES FOR GODLY LIVING

Our privilege: 2 Pe 1:3
- related to God as Father   (1 Jn 3:1 + 2)
- engrafted into Jesus as the vine   (Jn 15:5)
- indwelt by the Holy Spirit   (Jn 14: 16 + 17)
    (see also Ac 1:8, Gal 5:22 + 23, 1 Co 12:4 + 11)
- endowed with divine nature   (2 Pe 1:4, Eph 4:24)
- provided with divine truth   (see Tit 1:1, 1 Ti 6:3)
- permitted direct prayer access   (Jn 16:23 + 24; Ps 32:6, 1 Ti 2:1 + 2)
- linked by faith   (see Ro 5:1–2, Gal 2:20)

F. THE NEED FOR TRAINING IN GODLINESS

Our responsibility: 1 Ti 4:7
- it takes determination   (see 1 Ti 6:11 KJV, Ps 101)
- it takes discipline   (see 2 Pe 1:5–7) ·
- it takes daily practice   (see Lk 9:23, Heb 5:14)
- it takes life-long progression   (see Php 3:12, 1 Jn 3:2)
- it takes obedience to God's revelation   (see 2 Ti 3:16)
- it takes co-operation with God's enabling grace   (see Tit 2:11 + 12, Col 2: 6 + 7)
- it takes God's power to bring about growth   (see Col 2:19, Php 4:13)

G. GODLY LEADERSHIP EMINENTLY DISPLAYED BY EZRA

Ezra 7 to 10 illustrates several key traits of a godly leader:
- focus on God's Word   (7:6 + 10 + 11)
- prayer   (8:23, 9:6–15)
- integrity   (7:10)
- anointing   (7:9 + 28)
- identifying with God   (see 9:6–10:1, 10:6)
- setting the example   (see 9:3, 10:1)
- refusing compromise   (see 10:3 + 10 + 11)
- taking action   (see 10:5 + 10 + 16)

Because of his godliness, Ezra had a profound impact on the lives of those whom he led

For further consideration:
     In your opinion, what is the connection between living a godly life and 'walking with God'? (see e.g. Ge 5:22 + 24, 6:9, 17:1, 48:15; also Col 2:6 NAS and Gal 5:16 + 25)

3

The Servanthood Principle

'... I am among you as the one who serves.'
(Lk 22:27, NAS)

A. SPIRITUAL LEADERSHIP ESSENTIALLY MEANS SERVANT-LEADERSHIP

A true leader will endeavour to serve his followers:
- by putting their interests above his own
- by seeking their fulfilment
- by helping implement their vision
- by promoting their progress

B. JESUS STRONGLY EMPHASIZED THE NEED FOR SERVANT-LEADERSHIP

- through His teaching:
    - Mt 20:20–28, Mk 9:33–37; Mt 23:1–12
    - Jn 12:24–26, 13:12–17
- through His example:
    - Isa 42:1–4, 52:13–53:12; Php 2:7 + 8, 1 Jn 3:16
    - Lk 22:27, Jn 10:10 + 11
    - Jn 13:1–11, 21:9–13; Mt 20:29–34, Lk 7:11–15

C. CHARACTERISTICS OF A TRUE SERVANT

- humble, submissive; reticent; modest
- unselfish; self-denying, sacrificing; giving
- available; sensitive; caring, supportive
- dedicated; disciplined; diligent, faithful
- remarkable servants in the Bible:[5]
    - ex. Abigail   (1 Sa 25:14–35)
    - ex. Barzillai   (2 Sa 17:27–29, 19:31–40)
    - ex. Araunah   (2 Sa 24:18–25)
    - ex. Tabitha   (Ac 9:36–41)

D. SERVANTHOOD UNDER SCRUTINY

A crucial test for genuine servanthood is the challenge to respond in the opposite spirit
– Scriptural guidelines:
    Pr 25:21 + 22, Mt 5:38–48, Ro 12:14 + 17–21, 1 Pe 3:9–18
– Scriptural examples:
    ex. Joseph   (Ge 50:15–21)
    ex. Elisha   (2 Ki 6:20–23)
    ex. Jesus   (Lk 23:34, 1 Pe 2:23)
    ex. Paul   (1 Co 4:12 + 13)

E. PERILS FOR SERVANTS TO GUARD AGAINST

– being dominated by the expectations and claims of others
– exhibiting a reluctance to say 'no'
– becoming a people-pleaser
– neglecting personal priorities
– majoring on secondary issues
– turning bitter because of feeling used, disrespected or unappreciated
– finding identity and security in service rather than in Christ

F. IN GOD'S KINGDOM, GREATNESS AS A LEADER EQUALS GREATNESS AS A SERVANT

– such greatness is not related to fame, power, success or status
– such greatness is not measured by how many are serving you, but by how many you are serving
– the paradox of greatness through servanthood: the way up is the way down (Mk 9:35, 10:43 + 44; Lk 6:38, Ac 20:35; Lk 17:33, Jn 12:24)
– the nobility of servanthood:
    the term 'servant of God' appears to be *the* favoured term of honour in the Scriptures for all those who fulfilled leadership roles in God's kingdom; see e.g. Ge 26:24, Nu 12:7, 14:24, 2 Sa 7:5, Mt 12:18; similarly, Tit 1:1, Jas 1:1

For further consideration:
    Trace how Paul is characterized as a servant leader through Ac 26:16, Ro 1:1, 2 Co 4:5, 1 Co 9:19, 2 Co 12:15, 1 Th 2:7–12, Ac 20:34 + 35 and 28:3

4

The Imitation Principle

'I have set you an example that you should do as I have done ...'
(Jn 13:15, NIV)

A. A SPIRITUAL LEADER MOST POWERFULLY LEADS THROUGH HIS EXAMPLE

- his model can direct   (see Jdg 7:17–20)
- his model can motivate   (see Mt 14:25–28)
- his model can influence behaviour
    - for good   (see 1 Ch 29:3–9 + 17, Lk 11:1; 1 Ti 4:12)
    - for bad   (see Ge 25:28 and 37:3, 1 Ki 15:34, 2 Ki 17:41)

B. SOME BASIC PRINCIPLES

- A leader must sow (through his example) what he desires to reap (through his followers' imitation of himself)
- Setting an example for imitation is the simplest and most natural way of shaping human character and action
- Imitation based on association produces formation.
    (see Pr 27:17, Mk 3:14; Pr 13:20; 1 Co 15:33, Pr 22:24 + 25, 26:4)
- Followers are more motivated to imitate their leader because of who he is than because of what he does

C. UNIQUE CHALLENGES OF SPIRITUAL LEADERSHIP

- to imitate God by following Jesus' example   (see Eph 5:1 + 2)
- to cultivate traits worth emulating   (see 2 Pe 1:5–8, 1 Pe 5:1–3)
- to establish a godly prototype suitable
  for reproduction   (see Heb 13:7, 2 Ti 2:2)

D. THE IMITATION PRINCIPLE POINTED OUT

- by Jesus: e.g. Lk 6:40, 9:23, Jn 5:19 + 20, 8:26, 12:45, 13:34, 15:12
- by Peter: e.g. 1 Pe 1:15 + 16, 2:21–24, 4:1, 5:2 + 3, 2 Pe 2:6
- by John: e.g. 1 Jn 1:1–5, 3:2, 3:16, 4:11 + 19, 3 Jn 11
- by Paul: e.g. Ro 4:12, 1 Co 4:16 + 17, Php 3:17, 1 Th 2:14, 2 Th 3:6–9,
                2 Ti 1:13, Tit 2:7

E. BIBLICAL IMAGES FOR THE IMITATION PROCESS

– learning from Jesus   (Mt 11:29, see also Eph 4:20)
– following in Jesus' footsteps   (1 Pe 2:21)
– walking as Jesus walked   (1 Jn 2:6)
– patterning after Jesus   (see 1 Ti 1:16, KJV)
– thinking like Jesus   (see Php 2:5)

F. JESUS IS THE GODLY EXAMPLE TO BE IMITATED

– He emulated His Father   (Jn 5:19, 12:50, 15:9)
– Thus, He set the perfect godly model   (Jn 1:18, 14:9, Heb 1:3)
– The Scriptures obligate us to imitate Him in character and action
     (see e.g. Mt 16:24, Php 2:5–8, Col 3:13, Heb 12:2 + 3; Jn 13:14 + 15,
     Mt 28:19 + 20)

Notice:
     To imitate Jesus does not mean to strive, through fleshly endeavour, to copy
     Him; but rather, to receive His abiding presence which, through the Holy Spirit,
     reproduces His likeness in us (see Jn 15:4 + 5, Col 2:6; 2 Co 3:18)

G. THE INTENDED IMITATION PROCESS ILLUSTRATED IN PAUL'S MINISTRY

– Paul imitated Jesus' example
     (1 Co 11:1; Mt 4:23 and Ac 28:31, Mk 3:14 and Ac 16:3, Mk 1:23–26 and
     Ac 16:16–18)
– Paul set the Christ-like example for his followers to imitate
     (1 Co 11:1; Php 4:9, 2 Th 3:9, 2 Ti 3:10 + 11)
– Their imitation secured the continuation and multiplication of authentic
     Christ-like living
     (see 2 Co 3:2 + 3, 1 Th 1:6 + 7, 4:1, 2 Ti 3:14, 2 Co 12:18)

For further consideration:
     As a leader, setting an example worth emulating does not equal living in a state
     of perfection; reflect upon David's life (e.g. 1 Sa 13:14, Ps 78:70–72; 2 Sa 11, Ps 51,
     2 Sa 24; 1 Ki 9:4)

Nothing determines the confidence people have in their leader
more than his character.
DEREK PRIME (6)

... when God raises up a man for special service He first works
in that man the principles which later on are, through his
labours and influence, to be the means of widespread blessing
to the Church and to the world.
D.E. HOSTE (7)

A.

SETTING AN EXAMPLE
AS
A MAN OF GOD-PLEASING ATTRIBUTES

5

Fear of God

'and he will delight in the fear of the LORD.'
(Isa 11:3, NIV)

A. THE REQUIREMENT

– The Scriptures command us to fear God   (Dt 6:24, 10:12 + 13, Ecc 12:13)
– All the world is to fear God   (Ps 33:8, 67:7)

B. THE REALIZATION

As God's children, we need not be afraid of our heavenly Father
    – He loves us (1 Jn 4:8 + 16, Jn 3:16, 1 Jn 3:1, 4:18)
    – we approach Him, as adopted children, not with a fearful but with a
      confident attitude (see Ro 8:14–16, Gal 4:6; 2 Ti 1:7)
To fear God essentially implies to render Him due awe and reverence
    (Dt 28:58, 1 Ch 16:25, Ps 22:23, Heb 12:28 + 29, Rev 14:7, 19:5)
Men ought to dread God as the judge of all sin
    (Ecc 8:12 + 13, Lk 12:5, 1 Pe 1:17, Php 2:12, Heb 10:27 + 31, Rev 11:17 + 18)

C. THE REASONABLENESS

To fear God is the adequate response to the excellency of His character.
e.g. – He is the Lord of lords   (Ps 136:3, Jer 10:6 + 7)
     – He is the mighty Creator   (see Ps 136:5–9, Jer 5:22 + 24)
     – He is the God of signs and wonders   (Ps 105:27–41, 136:4)
     – He is the God of majesty   (Ps 93:1, 1 Ch 29:11)
     – He is the Holy One   (Pr 9:10, Rev 15:3 + 4)
Fearing God clarifies man's position before Him   (see 2 Co 6:16–7:1)
Godly fear is meant to prevent sin   (Ex 20:20, Pr 8:13)
Fearing God helps develop proper relationships   (see Lev 25:17, Eph 5:21)
Godly fear is true wisdom   (Mic 6:9, Job 28:28)

D. THE REALITY

ex. Noah	(Heb 11:7, NAS)	ex. Obadiah	(1 Ki 18:3 + 12)
ex. Abraham	(Ge 22:12)	ex. Hezekiah	(Jer 26:19)
ex. Joseph	(Ge 42:18)	ex. Ezekiel	(see Eze 44:4)

E. THE REWARD

– God's friendship   (Ps 25:14)
– God's abundant goodness   (Ps 31:19)
– God's mercy   (Lk 1:50)
– God's compassion   (Ps 103:13, NAS)
– God's help   (Ps 115:11)
– God's guidance   (Ps 25:12)
– God's provision   (Ps 34:9, 111:5)
– wisdom   (Ps 111:10, Pr 15:33)
– answered prayer   (see Heb 5:7, Ne 1:11)
– protection from evil   (Pr 16:6)
– work blessings   (Ps 128:1 + 2)
– family blessings   (Ps 128:3 + 4, 112:1 + 2)
(Moreover, see Ps 33:18, 34:7, 145:19, 61:5, 115:13, Pr 1:7, 22:4, 14:26, 10:27, 28:14)

F. REMEMBER

– God delights in whoever fears Him   (Ps 147:11, see also Ac 10:35)
– Godly fear must be learned   (Dt 4:10, 31:12 + 13, Ps 34:11)
– We should pray for the fear of God   (see Ps 86:11)
– God is willing to place godly fear into our hearts   (see Jer 32:40)
– The Holy Spirit conveys a spirit of the fear of God (see Isa 11:2)

For further consideration:
   What can be learned about a God-fearing life-style from Job's example as
   outlined in Job 1:1 + 8, 1:9–11, 1:22, 2:3, and 2:10?

6

Humility

'... I am ... humble in heart ...'
(Mt 11:29, NIV)

A. MARKS OF HUMILITY

- Humility is the acknowledgment of man's true position before his Creator
- Humility is the appropriate response to God's holiness, perfection and love
- Humility is the justified appraisal of one's God-given talents and responsibilities
- Humility is the willingness to be known before men as known by God
- Humility is the gateway to honour in God's kingdom   (see Mt 18:4, Pr 15:33)
- Humility is a divine requirement   (Mic 6:8)

B. QUALITIES OF THE HUMBLE PERSON

– modesty	ex. Daniel	(Da 5:16 + 17)
– submissiveness	ex. Jesus	(see Mt 26:39)
– meekness	ex. Moses	(Nu 12:3)
– teachability	ex. Mary	(see Lk 10:39)
– servanthood	ex. Paul	(Ac 20:19)

C. GOD BLESSES THE HUMBLE

- Jas 4:6; Ps 25:9, 149:4, Pr 3:34, 22:4, 1 Pe 5:6
    - ex. Jacob   (Ge 32:9–12)
    - ex. David   (2 Sa 7:8–21)
    - ex. Jesus   (Php 2:5–11)
    - ex. Paul   (Eph 3:8)

D. PRIDE: A DANGEROUS TRAP, PARTICULARLY FOR LEADERS

- Pr 6:16 + 17; Ps 31:23, 18:27, Pr 16:18
    - ex. David   (see 1 Ch 21:1–4)
    - ex. Uzziah   (2 Ch 26:16)
    - ex. Hezekiah   (see 2 Ki 20:12–18, 2 Ch 32:31)

E. FEATURES OF PRIDE

– Pride directs the attention from God and others to self
– Pride expresses itself through complacency, haughtiness, presumption, jealousy,
    contempt, boasting, criticism, false humility, etc.
– Pride deceives and blinds to personal spiritual needs
– Pride is one of the enemy's prime target areas
        (see Ge 3:5, 1 Ch 21:1, Mt 4:8 + 9, Jn 6:15)

F. GOD RESISTS THE PROUD

– 1 Pe 5:5; Ps 18:27, Pr 15:25, 16:5; Isa 13:11
        ex. Lucifer   (Isa 14:12–15)
        ex. Haman   (Est 5:9–7:10)
        ex. Nebuchadnezzar   (Da 4:28–37, 5:18–21)
        ex. Herod   (Ac 12:21–23)

G. HUMBLING: THE RETURN ROUTE TO RESTORATION

– Jas 4:8–10, 2 Ch 7:14; see also Lk 18:13 + 14 and Isa 57:15 + 16
        ex. David   (1 Ch 21:7 + 8, see also Ps 51:1–17)
        ex. Hezekiah   (2 Ch 32:25 + 26)
        ex. Manasseh   (2 Ch 33:10–13)

H. HUMILITY AND PRIDE CONTRASTED

– Humility is God-centred, pride self-centred
– Humility is a root virtue, pride a root vice
– Humility enjoys dependence, pride independence
– Humility seeks to give, pride to get
– Humility conduces to spiritual growth, pride to spiritual decline

For further consideration:
    In which respects do Jn 1:19–34 and 3:28–30 highlight John the Baptist's great
    humility?

7

Obedience

'... I keep his word.'
(Jn 8:55)

A. WHAT OBEDIENCE IS

To obey God means to willingly respond to His wishes and demands
- God's claims on our lives are born out of His Fatherly love and wisdom
- Thus, true obedience is the intelligent choice to comply with God's loving intentions
- Obedience to God is never negotiable

Obedience is closely interrelated with:
- the fear of God   (see Dt 6:2, 8:6, 10:12 + 13, 1 Sa 12:14)
- salvation   (see Mt 7:21, Heb 5:9, Jn 3:36)
- faith   (see Ro 1:5, 16:26)
- love   (see 1 Jn 2:5, 5:3, 2 Jn 6)
- humility   (see Php 2:5–8)
- answered prayer   (see 1 Jn 3:22)

B. OBEDIENCE IS A KEY TO SPIRITUAL USEFULNESS

- It qualifies one to co-operate with God according to His desires and plans
- It is conducive to sanctification   (see 1 Pe 1:14 + 15 + 22, Ro 6:22)
- It is pre-conditional to receiving the Holy Spirit   (see Ac 5:32)
- It is essential for exercising spiritual authority (see Jos 1:1–9)

C. CORNERSTONES FOR TRUE OBEDIENCE

- God's work on the heart   (see Dt 30:6–10, Eze 36:27, Heb 13:20 + 21)
- responding out of love   (see Jn 14:15 + 23 + 31)
- submission   (see Jas 4:7, Heb 13:17, Tit 3:1)

D. DISTINGUISHED PORTRAITS OF OBEDIENCE IN THE SCRIPTURES

ex. Noah	(Ge 6:13–22,7:5 + 9 + 16)
ex. Abraham	(Heb 11:8, Ge 22:15–18)
ex. the Rechabites	(Jer 35:1–19)
ex. Jesus	

      – He sought God's will above His own   (Jn 5:30, 6:38, Lk 2:42)
      – He learned to obey   (Heb 5:8)
      – He obeyed joyfully   (see Ps 40:7 + 8, Jn 4:34)
      – He obeyed absolutely   (Jn 8:29)
      – He obeyed unto death   (Php 2:8)

E. WE REAP WHAT WE SOW

– fruits of obedience:
      – God's rich blessings   (see Dt 28:1–14, Ex 20:6)
      – security   (see Lev 25:18 + 19, 26:5)
      – peace   (see Isa 48:18)
      – success   (see Jos 1:7 + 8, 1 Ki 2:3)
– fruits of disobedience:
      – God's wrath   (see 2 Ch 34:21, Jn 3:36)
      – misery   (see Jer 29:17–19, 32:23 + 24)
      – bondage   (see 2 Ki 18:11 + 12, Ro 6:16–20)

F. THE SERIOUSNESS OF DISOBEDIENCE

– It disturbs the order of God's moral universe
– It hinders the purposes of God
– It promotes the interests of the powers of darkness
– It is viewed by God as abominable as witchcraft (1 Sa 15:23)
– It implies a disrespect for God's character and His rightful claims
– It is based on rebellion stemming from pride because of selfishness

For further consideration:
     Examine the warning examples of disobedience as seen in the lives of Moses and Aaron (Nu 20:2–13 + 14, Dt 32:48–52) and Saul (1 Sa 13:7–14, 15:17–23).

8

Integrity

'Can any of you prove me guilty of sin? ...'
(Jn 8:46, NIV)

A. INTEGRITY ESTABLISHED

God is a God of integrity
    (see Ps 92:15, Ge 18:25, Job 34:10–19, Ps 145:17, Dt 32:4)
The Lord Jesus lived a life of integrity
    (see 1 Pe 1:19, 2:22, Isa 53:9, Jn 18:23, 18:38, Lk 23:41)
Integrity is a Biblical standard, particularly befitting spiritual leadership
    (see 1 Pe 1:14–16, 1 Jn 2:6; Php 2:15; 1 Pe 5:2 + 3, 1 Ti 4:12; 3:2–13,
    Tit 1:5–9)

B. INTEGRITY DEFINED

– to be righteous	(see Mk 6:20, Lk 1:6)
– to be blameless	(see Ge 17:1, Eph 1:4)
– to be pure in heart	(see 1 Ti 1:5, Mt 5:8)
– to be upright	(see Tit 2:12, Job 1:1)
– to be truthful	(see Ps 51:6, 15:2; Mt 23:27 + 28)
– to practise justice	(see Pr 21:3, Dt 25:13–16)
– to lead a clean life	(see Ps 24:3 + 4, 1 Sa 29:3)

Note:
    Integrity does not mean perfection, but rather wholeness, the integrated oneness
    of inner life and outer action, congruence with God's standards of character and
    conduct.

C. INTEGRITY ILLUSTRATED

ex. Noah	(Ge 6:9)
ex. Samuel	(see 1 Sa 12:3–5)
ex. David	(1 Ki 9:4, Ps 7:8)
ex. Asa	(2 Ch 15:17)
ex. Paul	(1 Th 2:10, 2 Co 6:3–8)

D. INTEGRITY TESTED

A leader's integrity may be tested by:
God; fellow Christians; non-Christians, especially enemies of the things of God
Leaders whose integrity was tested:

ex. Joseph	(Ge 39:6–10)	ex. Job	(Job 1:8–12)
ex. Moses	(Nu 12:1–8)	ex. Daniel	(Da 6:4 + 5)
ex. Hezekiah	(2 Ch 32:31)	ex. Jesus	(Jn 8:6)

Major areas prone to come under scrutiny:
    commitment to God; morals; work and ministry performance; marriage and
    family life; handling of finances

E. INTEGRITY GUARDED

- the necessity of being watchful
        (see Lk 17:3, 21:34, Ac 20:28, 1 Ti 4:16, 2 Co 13:5; Ps 101:2)
- the necessity of determining to lead a life of integrity
        (see Mk 9:43–47, 2 Pe 3:14, Pr 4:23–27; Ps 119: 101, 101:1–8)
- the necessity of preserving a clear conscience
        (see 1 Ti 1:5, 3:9, 1 Pe 3:16; Ac 23:1, 24:16, Heb 13:18)
- the necessity of drawing upon the Holy Spirit's enabling impartation
        (see Ps 51:10, Eze 36:26 + 27; 2 Co 3:18, Gal 5:16–25; 2 Pe 1:3 + 4)

F. INTEGRITY REWARDED

- by God's guidance	(see Pr 11:3, Isa 26:7)
- by God's strengthening	(see 2 Ch 16:9, Job 17:9)
- by God's protection	(see Pr 2:7 + 8; Ps 25:21, Da 6:22)
- by God's answering prayer	(see Pr 15:29, 1 Jn 5:15, 3:21 + 22)
- by God's vindication	(see Ps 24:4 + 5; 26:1–12)

(see also Ps 119:1–3, 5:12, 84:11; Pr 28:10, 10:9, 28:18, 22:11, 21:21, 20:7)

For further consideration:
    As you study Ge 20, what does this chapter reveal about the measure of
    integrity in Abraham's and Abimelech's lives?

9

Faithfulness

'He was faithful to the one who appointed him ...'
(Heb 3:2, NIV)

A. FAITHFULNESS – A PROMINENT FEATURE OF GOD'S CHARACTER (Ex 34:6)

God's faithfulness is displayed e.g.
– in His steadfast love
    (Ps 100:5, 117:2, 25:10, 86:15, 89:2)
– through His fulfilling His promises
    (Ps 145:13, Heb 10:23, Jos 21:45, 1 Ki 8:56)
– by His continual willingness to forgive our sins
    (1 Jn 1:9, Ne 9:17)
– in His completing the work of our sanctification
    (1 Th 5:23 + 24, see also 1 Co 1:7–9)
– through His assistance in times of temptation
    (1 Co 10:13, see also 2 Th 3:3)
– in His meeting all our needs
    (see Php 4: 19, Mt 6:33)
– by His rewarding those who are faithful
    (see 1 Sa 26:23)

B. FAITHFULNESS DESCRIBED

This godly attribute is closely related to:
– trustworthiness   (see Ps 111:7 + 8, Ex 18:21)
– reliability   (see 1 Ti 2:13, Ge 48:15)
– loyalty   (see Pr 3:3, Ps 89:33)
– whole-heartedness   (see Jer 32:41, 2 Ki 20:3)
– diligence   (see Mt 25:21 + 23 + 26, Ex 15:26)
– consistency   (see Dt 7:9, Heb 13:8, Da 6:16 + 20)
– endurance   (see Mt 24:13, Lk 9:62)

C. BIBLICAL LEADERS OF OUTSTANDING FAITHFULNESS

ex. Abraham	(Ne 9:7 + 8)	ex. Hezekiah	(2 Ch 31:20)
ex. Moses	(Heb 3:5)	ex. Daniel	(Da 6:4)
ex. Joshua	(see Jos 24:14 + 15)	ex. Paul	(see 1 Ti 1:12)
ex. Samuel	(1 Sa 2:35)	ex. Timothy	(see 1 Co 4:17)
ex. David	(see 1 Ki 3:6)		

D. FAITHFULNESS – AN INDISPENSABLE REQUIREMENT FOR SPIRITUAL LEADERSHIP

The Bible repeatedly highlights this vital character trait, e.g. in
– Ps 31:23, 101:6; 78:8, 12:1
– Pr 20:6, 3:3, 19:22; 12:22; 28:20, 20:28; 14:22, 16:6
– Mt 25:14–30, Lk 19:11–27, Mt 24:45–51; Lk 16:10–13; Rev 2:10
– 1 Co 4:1 + 2; 2 Ti 2:10–13; 2:2, 1 Ti 3:11, Tit 2:2 + 10; Gal 5:22

According to the key passage Lk 16:10–12, spiritual responsibility can be confidently entrusted only if there has been proof of
– faithfulness in small things   (v.10)
– faithfulness in material matters   (v.11)
– faithfulness in handling someone else's affairs   (v.12)

E. LEADERS NEED TO MAKE FAITHFULNESS A PRIORITY

– in serving God   (see Heb 2:17, Col 4:7)
– in handling the Word of God properly   (see 2 Ti 2:15, Jer 23:28)
– in their commitment to prayer   (see Col 1:7 + 4:12)
– in employing their spiritual gifts   (see 1 Pe 4:10, 1 Ti 4:14)
– in shepherding the people entrusted to them   (see 1 Pe 5:2–4, Jn 21:15–17)
– in doing good   (see Gal 6:9, Ac 10:38)
– in their use of time   (see Eph 5:16)

For further consideration:
    Reflect upon faithfulness as a channel of blessing in the light of Pr 12:22, 28:20, 3:3 + 4, Ps 31:23 and Rev 2:10

10

Diligence

'... having loved his own who were in the world,
he loved them to the end.'
(Jn 13:1)

A. DILIGENCE IMPLIES DETERMINATION

ex. Jacob   (Ge 32:26)
ex. Jesus   (Lk 9:51)
– the importance of removing obstacles   (see Heb 12:1, Mk 4:16–19)
– the danger of lacking determination   (see 2 Ki 13:14–19)

B. DILIGENCE IMPLIES COMMITMENT

ex. Caleb   (Jos 14:6–14)
ex. Jesus   (Jn 9:4)
– God deserves our best   (see 2 Ti 2:15)
– the danger of complacency   (see Pr 1:32, Rev 3:17–19)

C. DILIGENCE IMPLIES EARNESTNESS

ex. Jesus   (Lk 22:44)
ex. Titus   (2 Co 8:16 + 17)
– earnestness in prayer   (see Jas 5:16 + 17)
– earnestness in seeking spiritual gifts   (1 Co 12:31)
– earnestness in defending the faith   (Jude 3, KJV)

D. DILIGENCE IMPLIES ZEAL

ex. Jehu   (2 Ki 10:15–28)
ex. Jesus   (Jn 2:13–17)
– we are to be zealous for God   (Ro 12:11)
– we are to be zealous for unity   (Eph 4:3)
– the danger of being over-zealous   (see 2 Sa 21: 1–6)
– the danger of being zealous for a wrong cause (see Php 3:6)

E. DILIGENCE IMPLIES CONSISTENCY

ex. Daniel	(Da 6:10)
ex. Jesus	(2 Th 3:5)
– consistency as a spiritual goal	(see 1 Ti 6:11)
– the danger of sluggishness	(see Pr 6:6–11, Heb 6:11 + 12)

F. DILIGENCE IMPLIES ENDURANCE

ex. Joshua	(Jos 8:18 + 26)
ex. Jesus	(Heb 12:2 + 3)
– endurance in trials	(Jas 1:12)
– endurance in suffering	(see Ro 5:3 + 4, 2 Ti 2:9–12)
– endurance when God disciplines	(Heb 12:7)
– endurance to inherit promises	(Heb 10:36, 6:15)
– God strengthens for endurance	(see Col 1:11–12)

G. DILIGENCE IMPLIES PATIENCE

ex. David	(Ps 40:1)
ex. Jesus	(1 Ti 1:16)
– patience in doing good	(see Ro 2:6 + 7)
– patience in forgiving	(see Lk 17:4)
– the need to put on patience	(Col 3:12 + 13, see also Eph 4:1 + 2)
– patience as a fruit of the Spirit	(Gal 5:22)

H. DILIGENCE – CHALLENGE AND BLESSING

– we are to excel in diligence   (see 2 Co 8:7, KJV)
– promises for the diligent:
   Pr 13:4, 21:5, 12:27, 12:24, 22:29 (KJV); Heb 11:6 (KJV)

For further consideration:
   Dt 6:4–7, 6:17, Jos 1:8, Eph 6:18 and Col 3:23 indicate major areas in which we
   ought to practise diligence. What are they?

11

Love

'As the Father has loved me, so have I loved you ...'
(Jn 15:9)

A. THE DIVINE EXAMPLE

God is love	(I Jn 4:8 + 16)
God's love is	
– universal	(see Jn 3:16, 1 Ti 2:4)
– unconditional	(see Ro 5:6–10)
– sacrificial	(see Ro 8:32, Eph 5:2)
– forgiving	(Ps 103:3, 1 Jn 1:9)
– consistent	(Dt 7:9)
– everlasting	(Ps 106:1)
God's love was manifested in the sending of His Son	(1 Jn 4:10)
God's love culminated on the cross	(see Jn 15:13, 1 Jn 3:16)
God's love was exemplified through Jesus	(see Jn 14:9, 15:9)
God's love is conveyed through the Holy Spirit	(Ro 5:5, see also Gal 5:22)

B. THE DESIRED HUMAN RESPONSE

1 Jn 4:19 states that God's love for us creates a response of love for Him

– loving God as the chief commandment	(Mt 22:38)
– loving God with the totality of our being	(Mk 12:30; see also Dt 13:3)
– loving Jesus as foundational to any ministry	(see Jn 21:15–17)
– loving Jesus evidenced through obedience	(Jn 14:21 + 23, 1 Jn 2:5)

1 Jn 4:11 emphasizes that God's love for us should create a response of love for others

– we should love as God loves	(Eph 5:1 + 2, Mt 5:44–48)
– we should love others as ourselves	(Mk 12:31, Mt 7:12)
– we should love as servants	(Gal 5:13)
– we should love by deeds	(1 Jn 3:17 + 18)

1 Jn 4:20 indicates that the quality of love for our brother reveals the quality of our love for God

C. THE UNSELFISHNESS OF GODLY LOVE

It doesn't lay down conditions
It doesn't withhold blessing
It doesn't shrink from sacrifice
It doesn't expect reciprocation
It doesn't covet praise
It doesn't give up

D. THE SPECTRUM OF GODLY LOVE

True love seeks expression in
– kindness
    ex. Jesus   (see Mk 10:13–16)   ex. Boaz   (Ru 2:8–16)
– meekness
    ex. Jesus   (Mt 11:29, KJV)   ex. Moses   (Nu 12:3)
– humility
    ex. Jesus   (Php 2:5–8)   ex. Jacob   (see Ge 32:10)
– truthfulness
    ex. Jesus   (Jn 8:45)   ex. Nathanael   (Jn 1:47)
– faithfulness
    ex. Jesus   (Isa 11:5)   ex. Job   (see Job 1:5)
– compassion
    ex. Jesus   (Mt 15:32; 14:14; Lk 7:13; Mk 6:34)
– mercy
    ex. Jesus   (Heb 2:17)   ex. Elisha   (see 2 Ki 6:21–23)
– patience
    ex. Jesus   (see Heb 12:3)   ex. David   (Ps 40:1)
– forgiveness
    ex. Jesus   (Lk 23:34)   ex. Stephen   (Ac 7:60)

For further consideration:
    With Ex 34:6 + 7 in mind, ponder over 1 Co 13:4–7.

Spiritual leadership can be exercised only by Spirit-filled men. Other qualifications for spiritual leadership are desirable. This is indispensable.
J. OSWALD SANDERS (8)

B.

**SETTING AN EXAMPLE
AS
A SPIRIT–ENDUED MAN**

12

Anointing for God's Service

'... God anointed Jesus of Nazareth with
the Holy Spirit and with power.'
(Ac 10:38)

A. ANOINTING UNDER THE OLD COVENANT

It signified, generally speaking,
- appointment by God   (see Ex 3:10, 2 Ch 22:7)
- consecration to God   (see Lev 8:12)
- confirmation of God's presence   (see Dt 31:23, Ezr 7:28)
- communication of God's Spirit   (see Jdg 3:9 + 10, 1 Sa 16:13)

It was bestowed upon
- priests   (see Ex 40:12–15)   – prophets   (see 2 Ki 2:9 + 15)
- judges   (see Jdg 11:29)   – certain other leaders (see Ge 41:38)
- kings   (see 2 Sa 23:1 + 2)

It could be weakened or even forfeited
ex. Saul   (1 Sa 16:14, 28:15 + 16)
ex. Samson   (Jdg 16:19 + 20)

B. ANOINTING UNDER THE NEW COVENANT

It signifies, more specifically,
- divine commissioning   (see Ac 1:8)
- divine authorizing   (see Mk 16:17)
- divine empowering   (see Lk 24:49)
- divine enabling   (see Eph 1:19, 2 Pe 1:3 + 4)
- divine equipping   (see 1 Co 12:4–11, Ro 12:6–8)
- divine enlightening   (see 1 Jn 2:27, 1 Co 2:12)
It was bestowed upon
ex. the Lord Jesus   (Lk 3:21 + 22, 4:1 + 14 + 18, Ac 4:27)
ex. the apostles   (Ac 2:1–4; 9:17, 13:9)
ex. the early church   (Ac 4:31, 8:14–17, 10:44, 13:52, 19:1–6)
It is available to every Christian   (Ac 2:36 + 39, see also Lk 11:9–13)

It should rest, in its fullness,
      upon every Christian   (Eph 5:18)
It is maintained through
– abiding in Jesus   (see Jn 15:4 + 5, 1 Jn 2:27 + 28)
– obedience   (see Ac 5:32)

C. THIS ANOINTING IS IMPARTED BY THE LORD JESUS

– Mt 3:11, Mk 1:8, Lk 3:16, Jn 1:33
– Jn 15:26, 16:7
– Ac 2:33, 1 Jn 2:20

D. THIS ANOINTING PROVIDES POWER FOR SERVICE

– power to lead a godly life   (see 2 Pe 1:3, Eph 3:20)
– power in testifying   (see Ac 4:33)
– power in preaching   (see Ac 2:37, 1 Co 2:4 + 5)
– power in teaching   (see Mt 7:28 + 29)
– power in prayer   (see Jn 11:41–44, Ac 4:24–31)
– power to do miracles   (see Lk 5:17, Ac 6:8, 19:11 + 12)
– power over satanic forces (see 1 Jn 4:4, Lk 4:36, Ac 13:8–11)
– power to lead people to God (see Ac 2:41, 5:12 + 14, 13:12)

E. THIS ANOINTING IS THE MOST ESSENTIAL PREREQUISITE FOR EFFECTIVE SPIRITUAL LEADERSHIP

– Spiritual objectives can only be achieved by spiritual means through spiritual people
– Every leader needs divine unction to carry out his divinely assigned function
    (see Jn 6:63, 15:5; Ac 1:4 + 5; 2 Co 3:5 + 6; Ac 6:3 + 5)
– God anoints those whom He appoints
– God's anointing on a leader draws people and motivates them to follow
    (see 2 Ch 15:9, Lk 6:17–19; Jos 1:16 + 17, Mt 4:18–22)

For further consideration:
    Appraise the relevance of prayer for moving in the Holy Spirit's anointing (see Jas 4:2, Lk 11:13, 1 Ch 4:10).

13

Equipping Believers for God's Service

'I am the good shepherd ...'
(Jn 10:11)

A. MINISTRY GIFTS

Eph 4: 11 + 12 states that Christ bestowed in particular five gifts – apostles, prophets, evangelists, pastors, teachers – to equip believers both for their work in God's service and for the edification of the Body of Christ

B. THE GIFT OF AN APOSTLE

ex. Jesus (see Heb 3:1)   ex. Andronicus and Junias (Ro 16:7)

Purpose:	to establish churches	
Focus:	he is concerned about evangelism	(see Ro 15:19 + 20)
	he is concerned about discipleship training	(see Ac 14:21 + 22)
	he is concerned about leadership development	(see Ac 14:23)
	his ministry carries recognizable divine authority	(see 2 Co 12:12)

C. THE GIFT OF A PROPHET

ex. Jesus (see Lk 24:19)   ex. Agabus (Ac 11:27 + 28)

Purpose:	to communicate divine revelation	
Focus:	he encourages and comforts	(see 1 Co 14:3)
	he exhorts and edifies	(see Ac 15:32)
	he sometimes foretells future events	(see Ac 21:10 + 11)
Danger:	to become critical, judging or even a messenger of doom	

D. THE GIFT OF AN EVANGELIST

ex. Jesus (see Lk 4: 18 + 19)   ex. Philip (Ac 21:8)

Purpose:	to proclaim the good news	
Focus:	he longs to win people for Christ	(see Ro 9:1–3)
	he is fixed in his message	(see Lk 24:46 + 47)
	he is flexible in his methods	(see 1 Co 9:19–22)

E. THE GIFT OF A PASTOR

ex. Jesus   (see Heb 13:20)   ex. Ephesian leaders   (see Ac 20:28, NIV)

Purpose: to look after the spiritual welfare of God's people
Focus: he feeds the flock   (see 1 Pe 5:2, KJV)
             he guards the flock   (see Ac 20:28–31)
             he protects the flock   (see Jn 10:11–15)
Danger: to be preoccupied with people's needs rather than with God Himself

F. THE GIFT OF A TEACHER

ex. Jesus   (see Jn 3:2)   ex. Paul   (1 Ti 2:7)

Purpose: to instruct in Scriptural truth
             he seeks to communicate the whole counsel of God   (see Mt 28:20)
             he seeks to lead Christians to maturity   (see Col 1:28)
             he seeks to combat error   (see Ac 18:28)
Danger: to be preoccupied with the contents rather than with the listeners

G. ON USING MINISTRY GIFTS

- They are supernatural enablings for various spiritual leadership functions
- Their efficiency depends on their usage in love
- A servant of God can move in more than one of these gifts   (see 2 Ti 1:11)
- To move in the path of one's gift(s) greatly enhances one's leadership
  performance

H. ON DISCOVERING YOUR MINISTRY GIFT(S)

- What are you especially motivated to do?
- What has God confirmed by His blessing so far?
- What do mature Christians encourage you to pursue?

For further consideration:
    Can you suggest ways in which the remaining ministry gifts   (see 1 Co 12:28)
    also contribute to the equipping of believers?

If God is to own the message, then it has to be delivered in language understood by the people and in words dictated by the Spirit.
STEPHEN F. OLFORD (9)

C.

SETTING AN EXAMPLE
AS
A MAN OF THE WORD

14

Preaching the Gospel

'... he went on through cities and villages,
preaching and bringing the good news of the kingdom of God ...'
(Lk 8:1)

A. THE POWER OF GOD'S WORD

- It is alive and active   (Heb 4:12)
- It is like a fire and a hammer   (Jer 23:29)
- it is the sword of the Holy Spirit   (Eph 6:17)
- It probes heart and mind   (Heb 4:12)
- It convicts   (see Ac 2:37)
- It regenerates   (1 Pe 1:23)
- It brings forth faith   (Ro 10:17)
- It doesn't return void   (Isa 55:11)
    (Moreover, see Eph 5:26, Ps 119:9 + 11, Ac 20:32, Ps 119:165, 2 Ti 3:16)

B. IMPORTANT FACETS OF THE GOSPEL MESSAGE

- the kingdom of God   (Lk 4:43, 9:2, Ac 8:12)
- repentance   (Mt 4:17, Lk 24:47)
- Christ's suffering   (Lk 24:46, Ac 17:3)
    - the centrality of the cross (1 Co 1:23, 2:2)
    - the power of the cross   (1 Co 1:18, see also Jn 12:32, Col 1:20)
- Christ's resurrection   (1 Co 15:3 + 4 + 14, Ac 17:3)
- justification by faith   (Mk 1:15, see also Ro 5:1)
- forgiveness of sins   (Lk 24:47, Ac 26:18)
- reconciliation with God   (see 2 Co 5:18–20)
- sonship   (Ro 8:14–16)
- the Great Commission   (Mk 16:15, Mt 24:14)
    (See also Eph 1:13, Ro 1:16, Ac 20:24, Eph 6:15, 2 Co 4:4)

C. GUIDELINES FOR WISE PREACHING

– Live what you preach
– Preach the Word, not merely about the Word
– Preach with your eyes on the cross
– Preach the good news
– Preach the whole counsel of God
– Preach in utter dependence upon the Holy Spirit
– Preach the truth in love
– Preach without raising any disputes
– Seek to appeal to the conscience
– Seek to convince the intellect
– Seek to challenge the will
– Urge for an immediate response to God
– Preach simply
– Preach practically
– Preach instructively
– Preach earnestly
– Preach directly
– Preach emphatically
– Preach boldly

D. PITFALLS TO AVOID

– to preach to please people
– to preach to impress with knowledge or rhetoric
– to preach without thorough preparatory study of the Scriptures
– to preach without a solid foundation of prayer
– to preach a shallow or cheap gospel

For further consideration:
    Which insights can be gained from John the Baptist's preaching ministry?

15

Teaching the Word of God

'... and crowds gathered to him again;
and again, as his custom was, he taught them.'
(Mk 10:1)

A. THE NEED TO BE TAUGHT BY GOD

– on various aspects of His purposes for our lives e.g.
- His Word   (Ps 119:18)
- His statutes and precepts   (Ps 119:26 + 27)
- His ways   (Ps 25:4, see also 103:7)
- His will   (Ps 143:10)
- wisdom   (Ps 51:6, see also 90:12)
- understanding   (Ps 119:73 + 169)
- knowledge   (Ps 119:66)
- good judgment   (Ps 119:66)

– through the Holy Spirit
- Jn 14:26, 16:13–15; Lk 12:12; 1 Co 2:9–13
- 1 Jn 2:27
    (See also Ex 35:30–36:2)

B. TWO MAIN GOD-ORDAINED TEACHING ENVIRONMENTS

– the home
    Eph 6:4, Dt 6:7, 4:9 + 10, Pr 6:20–23, Ps 44:1
– the church
    1 Co 4:17, Eph 4:11 + 12, Col 3:16, Ro 15:14, Tit 2:1–5

C. PURPOSES OF BIBLICAL TEACHING

- to provide spiritual nourishment   (see 1 Ti 4:6, Col 2:7)
- to promote maturity   (see Heb 5:12–6:2)
- to protect against false teaching (see 2 Pe 2:1, Ac 20:30)
- to confute opposing views   (Tit 1:9)
- to equip believers for ministry   (see Eph 4:11 + 12)

D. HINDRANCES FOR BIBLICAL TEACHING TO TAKE ROOT

– lack of understanding	(Mt 13:19)
– a shallow commitment to the truth	(Mt 13:20 + 21)
– worldly-mindedness	(Mk 4:19)
– unbelief	(see Jn 5:38–40)
– spiritual insensibility	(Heb 5:11)

E. GUIDELINES FOR WISE TEACHING

– derived from Jesus' ministry:

– He taught by personal example	(Mt 11:29, Jn 13:12–15)
– He taught by principles	(Mt 5:1–11)
– He taught through stories (parables)	(Mk 4:1–9)
– He taught simply	(see Mt 13:45 + 46)
– He taught considerately	(Mk 4:33, see also Jn 16:12)
– He taught with authority	(Mt 7:29, see also Jn 7:16–18)
– He taught His disciples to teach	(Mt 11:1, 28:19 + 20)

– derived from Paul's writings:

– integrity indispensable	(Tit 2:7)
– life and teaching should correspond	(see Ro 2:17–24, 1 Co 4:6)
– adequate grasp of subject needed	(see 1 Ti 1:7)
– wisdom required	(Col 1:28, 3:16)
– doctrine must be sound	(Tit 2:1)
– church leaders should be apt to teach	(Tit 1:9, 1 Ti 3:2)
– teaching fundamental in developing leaders	(2 Ti 2:2)

For further consideration:
  In what respects does Apollos (Ac 18:24–28, 1 Co 4:6) exemplify traits of an outstanding teacher?

In nothing should the leader be ahead of his followers more
than in the realm of prayer.
J. OSWALD SANDERS (10)

... a leader's work needs to be born out of prayer in every area of
life and at every point of activity.
CHARLES SIBTHORPE (11)

D.

SETTING AN EXAMPLE
AS
A MAN OF PRAYER

16

Seeking God

'... he went out into the hills to pray; and all night he continued
in prayer to God. And when it was day, he called his disciples,
and chose from them twelve.'
(Lk 6:12 + 13)

A. SEEKING GOD – WHY?

– to fulfil one of the purposes of our existence	(Ac 17:26 + 27)
– out of heart desire	(Ps 63:1)
– it is commanded	(Ps 27:8)

B. SEEKING GOD – WHEN?

– at all times	(1 Ch 16:11)
– while God may be found	(Isa 55:6)
– in time of need	(Ps 77:2)
– now	(see Hos 10:12)

C. SEEKING GOD – HOW?

– whole-heartedly	(Ps 119:10, Jer 29:13)
– with earnestness	(see Ps 78:34)
– with total commitment	(see 2 Ch 15:12–15, 7:14)
– God Himself, not merely His blessings	(Jer 29:13, see also 1 Ch 16:11)

D. SEEKING GOD – LEADERS AT THE FOREFRONT

ex. Joshua	(see Jos 7:6–9)
ex. David	(2 Sa 21:1, Ps 27:8)
ex. Jehoshaphat	(2 Ch 17:4, 22:9)
ex. Hezekiah	(2 Ch 31:21)
ex. Ezra	(Ezr 8:21–23)
ex. Daniel	(Da 9:3)

E. SEEKING GOD – SERIOUS CONSEQUENCES OF ITS NEGLECT

ex. Israelites of Joshua's day	(Jos 9:14–22)
ex. Rehoboam	(2 Ch 12:14)
ex. Asa	(2 Ch 16:12)

F. SEEKING GOD – EVOKING MANIFOLD BLESSINGS

– God's presence	(see Ps 9:10)
– God's grace	(see 2 Ch 30:18–20)
– God's goodness	(La 3:25)
– God's provision	(Ps 34:10)
– God's answer	(see Ps 34:4)
– life	(see Am 5:4 + 6)
– righteousness	(Ps 24:5, KJV)
– understanding	(see Pr 28:5)
– peace	(see 2 Ch 14:7)
– success	(see 2 Ch 17:3–5, 26:5, 31:21)

G. SEEKING GOD – FINDING GOD

– Dt 4:29, 1 Ch 28:9, Jer 29:13 + 14; Mt 7:7 + 8
– Isa 65:1
– 2 Ch 15:4 + 15

H. GOD SEEKING

– fellowship	(see Ge 3:8, Jer 3:19-22)
– to save the lost	(Eze 34:16; Lk 19:10)
– men after His own heart	(1 Sa 13:14, see also 2:35)
– worshippers	(Jn 4:23)
– intercessors	(see Eze 22:30)

For further consideration:
   Meditate on Ps 14:1–5 and Ro 3:10–18

17

Interceding for Others

'I pray for them ...
for those you have given me ...'
(Jn 17:9, NIV)

A. INTERCESSION DEFINED

- to step in between
- to stand in the gap
- to function as mediator
- to represent the needs and interests of others before God
- to plead with God for someone else

B. LEADERS STANDING IN THE GAP FOR OTHERS

ex. Abraham	for Sodom and Gomorrah	(Ge 18:20–32)
ex. Moses	for the Israelites	(Ps 106:23)
ex. Samuel	for the people of Israel	(1 Sa 12:23)
ex. Job	for his friends	(Job 42:8–10)
ex. Jesus	for Simon Peter	(Lk 22:31 + 32)
ex. Paul	for the Ephesians	(Eph 1:16–21)

C. REASONS FOR INVOLVEMENT IN INTERCESSION

– to satisfy the longing of God's heart	(see Ez 22:30, Isa 59:16, 64:7)
– to co-operate with the Lord Jesus	(see Heb 7:25, Ro 8:34)
– to help extend the kingdom of God	(see Mt 6:10, 9:37 + 38)
– to enforce Christ's victory over Satan	(see 1 Jn 3:8, Col 2:15)
– to see people's needs met	(see Mt 7:7, Php 4:6)
– to grow in knowledge of God and His ways	(see Jer 33:3)
– to obey God's command	(see 1 Ti 2:1)

D. INTERCESSION AS A PRIESTLY OFFICE

- see Ex 28:9–12
- see Heb 7:24 + 25, 9:24; Jn 17:1–26
- see 1 Pe 2:5 + 9, Rev 1:6

E. BUILDING BLOCKS FOR POWER IN INTERCESSION

– holiness	(1 Ti 2:8, see also Ps 24:3–5)
– the help of the Holy Spirit	(Ro 8:26 + 27, see also Zec 4:6)
– knowing God's character and Word	(Ps 9:10, see also 119:105)
– discerning God's will	(1 Jn 5:14 + 15, see also Jn 10:27)
– faith	(Mk 11:22–24)
– obedience	(see 1 Jn 3:22)
– knowing how to deal with the enemy	(see Mt 12:29, 2 Co 10:3–5)
– the willingness to labour in prayer	(see Col 4:12, KJV; Gal 4:19)

F. SOME MAJOR AREAS FOR INTERCESSION

- the family
- the church
  e.g. unity, revival, maturity, spiritual leaders, missionary vision and commitment, the suffering and persecuted church
- the government
  e.g. peace, righteousness, justice, hunger after God
- the educational system
- the worlds of business, entertainment and the media
- the poor and needy, the sick and lonely
- the task of world evangelization
  e.g. the nations of the world, labourers for God, open doors for the gospel, people to be saved, growth of converts, people groups still unreached

For further consideration:
   Which intercession principles can be discerned in Nehemiah's prayer in Ne 1:5–11?

The leader is able to lead others because he has conquered himself.
J. OSWALD SANDERS (12)

Domination by the Holy Spirit makes possible the self-control that God and good leadership require.
JOHN HAGGAI (13)

E.

**SETTING AN EXAMPLE
AS
A MAN OF SELF-CONTROL**

18

Monitoring the Thought Life

'and you shall love the Lord your God ...
with all your mind ...'
(Mk 12:30)

A. WE ARE WHAT WE THINK (Pr 23:7, NAS)

– Thoughts develop into thought patterns
– Thought patterns mould actions
– Actions form habits
– Habits shape character

B. THE MIND IS A BATTLE-GROUND

– defects of the unregenerate mind
   (see Eph 4:18, 2 Co 4:4, Tit 1:15, 1 Ti 6:5)
– even with the born-again Christian, Satan continually attempts to influence
  his mind
   – he seeks to destructively infiltrate the thought life, desiring evil responses
     to be the result
      (see Ge 3:15, 2 Co 11:3; Mt 4:3 + 6 + 9)
   – he applies a variety of strategies to lead men astray
      (see e.g. 2 Co 2:11, Eph 6:11; 2 Co 11:13 + 14, 1 Ti 4:1)
– the conflict between flesh and spirit affects the mind
   (see Ro 8:3–13, Gal 5:16–25)
– the regenerate mind
   – the need to guard against conforming to worldly standards and practices
      (see Ro 12:2, 1 Pe 1:14)
   – the need to be progressively transformed in the mind
      (see Ro 12:2, Eph 4:23)
   – the need to flee from any temptation towards evil
      (see Mt 6:13; 2 Ti 2:22, 1 Co 6:18)
   – the need to actively resist the enemy
      (see Jas 4:7, 2 Co 10:3–5)

C. MEANS DESIGNED TO ENABLE US TO WIN THE BATTLE

– watchfulness
  (see 1 Pe 1:13, 5:8, 1 Co 10:12, Pr 4:23–27, 16:17)
– the help of the Holy Spirit
  (see 2 Co 3:18, 2 Ti 1:7, Eph 3:20; Gal 5:22 + 23; Eph 5:18)
– the Word of God
  (see Eph 6:17; Ps 119:9 + 11; Mt 4:4 + 7 + 10; Dt 8:3; Pr 7:1–3, Dt 6:6; Php 4:8, Ps 1:2)
– prayer
  (see 1 Th 5:17, Lk 18:1; Jas 4:2; Ps 139:23 + 24; 51:1 + 2 + 10 + 11)
– faith
  (see Col 3:5–9, Eph 4:22 + 31; Col 3:10 + 12–14, Eph 4:24 + 32; 6:16; Php 4:13)
– obedience
  (see Jn 13:17, Jas 1:22 + 25, Jos 1:8)

D. VITAL TO REALIZE

God knows our thought life	(Ps 139:2)
God knows our limitations	(Ps 103:13 + 14, Heb 4:15)
God is able to do what we can't do	(Jude 24, Heb 13:20 + 21)
God is committed to sanctify us completely	(1 Th 5:23 + 24)

For further consideration:
  Relative to the desire to possess a God-pleasing thought-life, how would you
  interpret the exhortations in Eph 6:10 and 2 Ti 2:1?

19

Bridling the Tongue

'When he was accused by the chief priests and the elders,
he gave no answer.'
(Mt 27:12, NIV)

A. THE CHALLENGE

– to let our speech be exemplary	(see 1 Ti 4:12)
– to let our speech be always gracious	(Col 4:6)
– to let our speech be in the name of Jesus	(Col 3:17)

B. AS THE HEART, SO THE TONGUE

– The mouth voices what is in the heart	(Lk 6:45)
– A righteous heart produces good talk	(Ps 37:30, Pr 10:11)
– A wicked heart produces evil talk	(Ps 10:3 + 7, Pr 24:1 + 2)
– Leaders must not be double-tongued	(1 Ti 3:8, see also Jer 9:8)

C. THE TONGUE EXERTS DESTRUCTIVE INFLUENCE

– when we speak carelessly
   Mt 12:26, Eph 5:6; 2 Co 12:20; Eph 5:4; 2 Ti 2:16 + 17; Pr 12:18
– when we voice discontent
   Jude 16; see also Nu 14:2, 1 Sa 20:30–34, Jnh 4:1–4
– when we speak in pride
   2 Co 12:20, Jas 4:16; Jude 18; Ps 73:8; Pr 17:5
– when our words damage relationships
   Pr 11:9; 16:28; 17:9; 15:1; 29:8; 19:13

D. THE TONGUE EXERTS CONSTRUCTIVE INFLUENCE

– when we speak the truth
   Eph 4:15; Mt 5:37; Dt 23:23; Ex 20:16, Pr 12:17
– when we make edifying remarks
   Eph 4:29; 1 Th 5:14, Col 3:16; Pr 10:21; 15:4; 15:30
– when we communicate blessing
   Pr 16:24, Job 16:5, Isa 50:4; Pr 12:25; 1 Co 4:12; Eph 5:19
– when our speech is to the glory of God
   Ps 109:30; 71:15, 35:28; 40:10; 119:172; 66:17
– when our words further relationships
   Pr 12:18; 10:10; 29:8; 12:6; 14:25; Ecc 10:12

E. GOD JUDGES THE USE OF THE TONGUE

– He knows all our words   (see Ps 139:4)
– He knows the heart attitude behind them   (see Jer 17:10, Ps 139:1–3)
– Our words will be judged   (see Mt 12:36 + 37, Ps 64:8)

F. GOD'S HELP IS NEEDED TO BRIDLE THE TONGUE

– We are exhorted to control the tongue   (see Jas 1:26, Ecc 5:2 + 6, Col 3:8)
– We are unable to do so in our own strength   (see Jas 3:8)
– We need divine assistance   (see Ps 141:3, 51:15, 120:2)
– A godly man controls his tongue   (see Job 2:10, Ps 17:3, Pr 15:28)

G. THE EXAMPLE OF THE LORD JESUS

– He spoke the truth   (Jn 8:45, 1 Pe 2:22)
– He spoke with grace   (Lk 4:22)
– He spoke with consideration   (see Jn 4:16–18)
– He spoke with compassion   (see Lk 7:13)
– He spoke with gentleness   (see Jn 8:10 + 11, Mk 10:38)
– He spoke with tenderness   (see Jn 21:15–17, Lk 10:41 + 42)
– He knew when not to speak   (see 1 Pe 2:23, Mt 27:14)

For further consideration:
   What bearing do Paul's remarks in 1 Co 13:4–7 have on the controlled use of the tongue?

20

Fasting

'And he fasted forty days and forty nights ...'
(Mt 4:2)

A. FASTING – A LOST KEY TO SPIRITUAL BLESSING

– Fasting was common in Bible times; for instance:
    ex. Moses   (Ex 34:28)
    ex. David   (Ps 69:10)
    ex. Nehemiah   (Ne 1:4)
    ex. Esther   (Est 4:16)
    ex. Daniel   (Da 9:3)
    ex. Anna   (Lk 2:37)
    ex. Paul   (Ac 9:9)
– In Mt 6:16, Jesus considered solely the 'when', not the 'if' of fasting
– Benefits of (regular) fasting are:
    – physical quickening
    – additional time before God
    – increase in prayer impact
    – special blessings released

B. VARIOUS KINDS OF FASTING

– normal fast (no food)
    ex. Jesus   (Lk 4:2)
– absolute fast (no food, no drink)
    ex. Ezra   (Ezr 10:6)
– partial fast (restricted diet)
    ex. Daniel   (Da 10:3)

C. ESSENTIAL: TO FAST UNTO THE LORD

To be effective, fasting needs to be practised in a way that is pleasing in God's sight:
– Zec 7:5
– Mt 6:16–18
– Isa 58:3–14

D. WE ARE ENCOURAGED TO FAST AND PRAY

- for personal consecration and sanctification
    - ex. Ezra   (Ezr 8:21)
- when in need of special direction
    - ex. Benjaminites   (Jdg 20:26–28)
    - ex. Antioch church leaders   (Ac 13:2)
- in order to receive divine revelation
    - ex. Daniel   (Da 9:2 + 3 + 21 + 22)
- for spiritual empowering
    - ex. Jesus   (see Lk 4:1 and 4:14)
    - ex. appointing early church elders   (Ac 14:23)
- to gain victory over powers of darkness
    - ex. Jesus   (Mt 4:1–11)
    - ex. the twelve disciples   (see Mk 9:29)
- to see national crises averted   (see Jer 18:7 + 8)
    - ex. Jehoshaphat   (2 Ch 20 + 3 + 4)
    - ex. Nineveh   (Jnh 3:4–10)
- to obtain a specific blessing needed
    - ex. Ezra   (Ezr 8:23)
    - ex. Antioch church leaders   (Ac 13:3)

For further consideration:
    How would you interpret the role of fasting in the event recounted in 2 Sa
    12:14–23?

Let parents be what they want their children to be.
ANDREW MURRAY (14)

F.

SETTING AN EXAMPLE
AS
A DEDICATED FAMILY MAN

21

Being a Blessing to your Family

'And Jesus said to him,
"Today salvation has come to this house ..." '
(Lk 19:9)

A. GODLY FAMILY GOVERNMENT

− an indispensable prerequisite for all spiritual leadership
    (1 Ti 3:4 + 12, Tit 1:6)
    − mismanagement of one's own household disqualifies for leadership
      within the Body of Christ (1 Ti 3:5)
    − what has not been learned and put into faithful practice at home,
      cannot be credibly applied in the church
− exemplified in the Scriptures by family heads like:

ex. Abraham	(Ge 18:19)	ex. Manoah	(Jdg 13:8)
ex. Jacob	(Ge 48:9 + 15)	ex. Job	(Job 1:5)
ex. Joshua	(Jos 24:15)		

B. A SCRIPTURAL RELATIONSHIP NETWORK

− the husband/father:
    − loves his wife   (Eph 5:25 + 28 + 33, Col 3:19)
    − is faithful to her   (see Mal 2:15, 1 Ti 3:2)
    − trusts her   (Pr 31:11)
    − honours her   (see 1 Pe 3:7, Pr 31:28)
    − is the head of his wife   (Eph 5:23, see also Ge 3:16)
    − is subject to her   (Eph 5:21)
    − loves his children   (see Pr 13:24)
− the wife/mother:
    − loves her husband   (Tit 2:4)
    − respects him   (Eph 5:33, 1 Pe 3:2)
    − is subject to him   (Eph 5:22−24, Col 3:18)
    − loves her children   (Tit 2:4)
− the children:
    − love their parents   (see Jn 19:26 + 27)
    − honour them   (Eph 6:2, see also 1 Ti 3:4)
    − obey them   (Eph 6:1, Col 3:20)

C. PRACTICAL RELATIONSHIP BUILDERS

As leader of the home, the husband/father can improve or deepen the
relationships with his wife and children through:
– sharing affection
– expressing gratitude, appreciation and encouragement
– being a good listener
– communicating well and frequently
– making family times a priority

D. ESSENTIAL LEADERSHIP FUNCTIONS OF THE FATHER

– He instructs his family from the Word   (see Eph 6:4)
   – on God's character   (see Isa 38:19, Ps 48:12–14)
   – on God's mighty deeds in the past   (see Dt 6:20–25, Ps 78:3 + 4)
   – on loving God   (Dt 6:4–9)
   – on obeying God   (Dt 32:46, Ps 78:5–8)
– He prays for the physical, mental, emotional and spiritual well-being
  of his family (see 1 Ti 2:8):
    ex. Isaac   (Ge 25:21, 27:27–30 + 28:1–4)
    ex. David   (2 Sa 7:19 + 25–29, 1 Ch 16:43)

E. TRAITS OF A GODLY FATHER THAT BRING BLESSING TO HIS FAMILY

– integrity	(Pr 20:7)	– mercy	(see Pr 21:21, KJV)
– righteousness	(Pr 3:33)	– diligence	(see Pr 10:4)
– love	(see Pr 10:12)	– prayerfulness	(see Pr 15:29)
– goodness	(Pr 13:22)	– obedience	(see Ge 26:3–5 + 24)
– faithfulness	(see Pr 28:20)		

F. IMPORTANT TO BEAR IN MIND

– God must build the home   (Ps 127:1)
– Fear of God is a key to great blessing in the home (Ps 128:1–4)
– No divided home will stand   (see Mt 12:25)

For further consideration:
    Which principle have Jos 24:15, Lk 19:9, Ac 11:14, 16:14 + 15, 16:31 + 34 and 18:8
    in common?

22

Bringing up your Children for God

'So it is not the will of my Father who is in heaven that one of
these little ones should perish.'
(Mt 18:14)

A. CHILDREN ARE A GIFT FROM GOD (Ps 127:3)

– The way in which we treat and train our children should mirror the way in
which God, as the perfect Father, treats and trains us   (see Eph 5:1)
– We are not merely to raise our children so they can earn a living; rather,
beyond that, the focus should be:
   – to help them get to know, love and obey God   (see Dt 6:4–7)
   – to disciple them into maturity in Christ   (see Ro 8:29)
– Spiritual leaders, in particular, are expected to bring up their
children for God   (see Tit 1:6, 1 Ti 3:4)

B. THE CHILDREN'S CHARACTER DEVELOPMENT AND SPIRITUAL GROWTH

– building-blocks of motivation:
      – the parents' example
      – the parents' intercession for their children
      – instruction from the Word of God
      – the Holy Spirit
– stumbling-blocks of rejection
      – a love deficit
      – lacking expressions of appreciation and encouragement
      – deprivation of attention and fellowship
      – criticism

C. WHAT A WISE PARENT DOES NOT DO

– He doesn't honour his child more than God
      ex. Eli   (1 Sa 2:12 + 29)
– He doesn't provoke his child to anger
      ex. Saul   (1 Sa 20:30–34)

– He doesn't tolerate his child's evil behaviour
    ex. David   (2 Sa 13:21)
– He doesn't withhold necessary discipline
    ex. Eli   (1 Sa 2:22–24, 3:13)
– He doesn't lead his child into sin
    ex. Rebekah   (Ge 27:5–17)
– He doesn't rob his child of future blessings
    ex. Solomon   (1 Ki 11:9–13)
– He doesn't prefer one child over another
    ex. Jacob   (Ge 37:3)

D. WHAT A WISE PARENT DOES

– He loves his child
    ex. Jairus   (Mk 5:22 + 23)
– He prays for his child
    ex. Jacob   (Ge 48:15 + 16)
– He teaches his child the things of God
    ex. Lois/Eunice   (2 Ti 1:5, see also 3:15)
– He seeks to keep his child in obedience
    ex. David   (1 Ki 2:3 + 4)
– He takes his child's needs seriously
    ex. Abraham   (Ge 24:2–4)
– He disciplines his child out of loving concern
    ex. God   (Heb 12:5–11)
– He forgives his child willingly
    ex. God   (1 Jn 1:9)

For further consideration:
    Which correlation of natural and spiritual growth is indicated in Lk 1:80, 2:40 and 2:52?

As we aim at being fruitful, we find our need of intelligent understanding of the Divine methods, in order that we may apply them in our own work.
J. HUDSON TAYLOR (15)

...unless men are willing to work like God works, they are going to encounter ruin down the line somewhere, with very little accomplished.
RALPH MAHONEY (16)

Good leaders do have a strategy.
It is essential, not optional.
DAVID L. HOCKING (17)

G.

SETTING AN EXAMPLE
AS
A MAN OF STRATEGY

23

Serving a God of Strategy

'... he has anointed me to preach good news to the poor. He has
sent me to proclaim release to the captives and recovering of
sight to the blind, to set at liberty those who are oppressed ...'
(Lk 4:18 + 19)

A. GOD IS A GOD OF STRATEGY

– divine strategy displayed through God the Father
  – His creation of the world   (Ge 1:1–31)
  – His plan of redemption   (Heb 1:1 + 2, Jn 3:16, Eph 1:4)
  – His dealings with the Israelites   (see Eze 20:1–44, 36:22–32)
  (generally, see Isa 46:9–11, Jer 29:11; more specifically, see 1 Ki 8:44:
  Jos 8:3, 10:11, Jdg 5:21, 1 Sa 14:15, 17:38–51, 2 Sa 5:17–25, 2 Ki 7:6 + 7,
  2 Ch 20:15–17)
– divine strategy manifested through the Holy Spirit, e.g.
  – Ac 11:12, 13:1–4, 16:6–10, 20:28
  – Eze 37:1, Mt 4:1, see also Jn 4:4
  – 1 Co 12:4–11; Ro 12:6–8; Eph 4:11–13, 1 Co 12:28
– divine strategy exemplified through the Lord Jesus, e.g.
  – His purposefulness   (Mt 20:28, Lk 19:10, 5:32, Jn 10:10)
  – His prayer strategy   (see Mt 6:9–13, Jn 17:1–26)
  – His preaching strategy   (see Mt 4:17, 10:7)
  – His discipleship strategy   (see Mk 3:14, Lk 6:40, Mt 28:19)
  – His outreach strategy   (see Mt 9:35–11:1)
  – His teaching strategy   (see Lk 10:1–16, Mk 3:27, Ac 1:8)

B. EFFECTIVE SERVICE TO GOD REQUIRES ABSOLUTE ADHERENCE TO GOD'S STRATEGY

Failure to seek God's specific direction spells disaster, e.g.
    ex. the Israelites   (Nu 14:40–45)
    ex. Joshua   (Jos 7:1–5, 9:14–16)
    ex. Jehoshaphat   (2 Ch 20:35–37)
Implementation of God's strategy secures blessing, e.g.
    ex. Moses   (Ex 14:15–31)
    ex. Joshua   (Jos 5: 13–6:21)
    ex. a poor widow   (2 Ki 4:1–7)

Especially when God's directions seem unusual or even contrary to human reasoning (see Isa 55:8 + 9, 1 Co 1:25–29), there is need for resolute obedience and unwavering faith, e.g.

ex. Gideon	(Jdg 7:2–8)
ex. Simon Peter	(Lk 5:4–7)
ex. a blind man	(Jn 9:6 + 7)

The Lord Jesus was utterly committed to His Father's strategy
  – Jn 6:38, 5:30, 4:34
  – Jn 5:19 + 20, 9:4, 5:36, 14:31, 17:4
  – Jn 14:24, 7:16, 8:26, 8:28, 12:49 + 50, 15:15, 17:8 + 14

C. THE CRUCIAL NECESSITY OF DOING GOD'S WORK GOD'S WAY

Only God-given strategy can expect the confirmation of God's full blessing
  – God-inspired strategy alone brings us fully into line with God's purposes
  – God-inspired strategy alone has divine impact
  – human wisdom alone is inadequate for achieving God's goals
  – human resources alone are no match for the powers of darkness
  – haphazard service misrepresents and dishonours God as a God of strategy
God desires to reveal His strategy to us
  – Ps 32:8 + 9, see also Isa 28:26
  – Jer 33:3, Jas 1:5
Scriptural means for discerning God's strategy

– prayer	(see Ps 25:4 + 5, 143:8, Pr 16:3)
– instruction from the Word	(see Ps 119:105; Mt 22:29)
– the leading of the Spirit	(see Jn 14:26, 16:13, 1 Co 2:9–11)

For further consideration:
  In what ways do the following passages throw light upon key aspects of Paul's missionary strategy: Ac 26:16–20, Ro 15:15–21, 1 Co 3:6–10, 9:19–23, 11:1, Col 1:28, 2 Ti 2:2, Ac 20:20 and Eph 6:10–20?

24

Living According to Priorities

'Now is my soul troubled. And what shall I say? "Father, save me from this hour"? No, for this purpose I have come to this hour.'
(Jn 12:27)

A. ESTABLISHING PRIORITIES

- Setting priorities means to decide which activities, opportunities, decisions, etc. are of primary importance
- In determining priorities, it is useful to ask: What is to be done first, next, at once, later, by someone else, not at all?
- Whatever helps us to best reach our goals should be considered a priority
- Once a priority has been set, it should not be violated
- We need to learn to say 'no' to what is not in line with our priorities
- We ought to invest our time in proportion to the order of our priorities
- Those who lead others must be especially careful in selecting their priorities

B. BEWARE

The good is the greatest enemy of the best
The urgent is the greatest enemy of the important

C. TOP PRIORITIES FOR ANY CHRISTIAN

– to love God	(Mt 22:37 + 38)
– to glorify God	(Eph 1:12–14, 1 Co 10:31)
– to seek God's kingdom and His righteousness	(Mt 6:33)
– to feed on God's Word	(see Mt 4:4)
– to pray	(1 Ti 2:1, Eph 6:18)
– to be filled with the Holy Spirit	(Eph 5:18)
– to pursue holiness	(Heb 12:14)
– to grow into Christ-likeness	(Ro 8:29)
– to lead a godly family life	(see Eph 5:21–6:4)
– to share the Gospel with all the world	(Mk 13:10, 16:15)
– to make disciples	(Mt 28:19)
– to rest	(see Ex 20:8–11, Mk 6:31)

D. ILLUMINATING CASE STUDIES IN THE SCRIPTURES

– manifestations of an inappropriate sense of priorities:

ex. Jonah:	disobedience	(Jnh 1:1–3)
ex. Martha:	over-busyness	(Lk 10:38–42)
ex. John and James:	ambition	(Mk 10:35–45)
ex. the young ruler:	materialism	(Mk 10:17–31)

– leaders who lived by clear priorities:

ex. Joshua:	relative to serving God	(Jos 24:14 + 15)
ex. David:	relative to praising God	(Ps 34:1)
ex. Ezra:	relative to God's Word	(Ezr 7:10)
ex. Jesus:	relative to prayer	(Mk 1:35, Lk 5:15 + 16)
	relative to God's will for His life	(Lk 22:42)
ex. Paul:	relative to his preaching technique	(1 Co 2:1–5)
	relative to his spiritual growth	(Php 3:7–14)

– leaders who solved problems with the help of clear priorities:

ex. Moses:	(Ex 18:13–27)	
– his problem:	overwork, exhaustion	(vv. 13 + 14 + 18)
– the solution:	setting new priorities	(vv. 19 + 20),
	delegating	(vv. 21 + 22 + 25 + 26)
– the result:	blessing for Moses and the people	(v. 23)

ex. the apostles:	(Ac 6:1–7)	
– their problem:	neglect of widows	(v. 1)
– the solution:	following the priorities set	(vv. 2 + 4)
	delegating	(vv. 3 + 5)
– the result:	further remarkable growth of the work	(v. 7)

For further consideration:
As you read Ac 16:6–10 and 2 Co 12:5–11, seek to discover how Paul had to adjust to God's priorities for each situation.

25

Strategizing a Project

'... Jesus said to Philip, "How are we to buy bread, so that these people may eat?" This he said to test him, for he himself knew what he would do.' (Jn 6:5 + 6)

A. STEP 1: RECEIVING A GOD-GIVEN VISION

ex. Moses (Ac 7:22–34)   ex. Nehemiah (Ne 2:12)
– Every vision needs time to mature
– Every vision is going to be tested

B. STEP 2: TAKING INVENTORY

ex. Nehemiah (Ne 2:13–15)   (see also Lk 14:28–32)
– What can *I* contribute to the fulfilment of the vision?
– What resources are required for the fulfilment of the vision?

C. STEP 3: SETTING GOALS

ex. Nehemiah (Ne 2:17)   ex. Jesus (Lk 4:18 + 19)
– A goal should be clear
– A goal should be measurable
– A goal should be attainable

D. STEP 4: ESTABLISHING PRIORITIES

ex. Jesus (Mt 10:5 + 6)   ex. Paul (Php 3:7–14)
– the necessary focus to set proper priorities: Mt 6:33
– the danger of responding to urgency rather than to importance

E. STEP 5: PLANNING

ex. David (1 Ch 28:2 + 11–21)   ex. Nehemiah (Ne 2:7 + 8)
– What is to be done?   (goals)
– How is it to be done?   (programme)
– When is it to be done?   (schedule)
– Who is to do it?   (personnel)
– What is the cost to do it?   (budget)

F. STEP 6: ORGANIZING

ex. Solomon (1 Ki 5:1–18)   ex. the apostles   (Ac 6:1–6)
– the need to define procedures
– the need to create structures
– the need to establish relationships

G. STEP 7: DIRECTING

– staffing   ex. David   (1 Ch 16:4–7)
– communicating   ex. Moses   (Nu 13:17–20)
– delegating   ex. Moses   (Ex 18:25 + 26)
– decision making   ex. Nehemiah   (Ne 4:7–23)

H. STEP 8: CONTROLLING

ex. Joshua (Jos 8:18 + 26)   ex. Jesus   (Jn 6:10 + 12; Mt 10:23)
– supervising if the work is proceeding as planned
– considering planning alternatives

I. STEP 9: EVALUATING

ex. Nehemiah (Ne 6:15 + 16)   ex. the disciples   (Mk 6:30, 9:28)
– Was the project carried out in obedience to the Spirit's leading?
– Has the original vision been fulfilled?
– Are the achieved results glorifying to God?
– Were lessons learned which can be helpful for future strategizing?

For further consideration:
   Seek to discern the above-mentioned nine stages in the development of Joseph's
   famine relief project (Ge 41:25–57, 45:6–8, 47:13–26).

... spiritual multiplication is far more effective in winning the world than is singular concentration on winning people. The effectiveness is not only in numerical growth but in quality of life in disciples and effectiveness of leadership.

CARL WILSON (18)

There is no greater leadership challenge than the challenge to help our followers become leaders capable of training their followers to be leaders also.

MYRON RUSH (19)

The real test of your leadership is whether or not other leaders are developed as you lead the way.

LEROY EIMS (20)

H.

SETTING AN EXAMPLE
AS
A MULTIPLIER

26

Discipling for a Worldwide Harvest

'And he appointed twelve, to be with him,
and to be sent out ...'
(Mk 3:14)

A. THE FRAMEWORK OF DISCIPLING

– God's global purposes
  (Ge 12:3, Isa 66:18–20, Rev 7:9; Jn 3:16 + 17, 1 Ti 2:4)
– Jesus' global perspective
    – relative to His personal mission
        (Jn 8:12, 8:26, 12:47, 12:32, 6:51, 17:21)
    – relative to the evangelization of the world
        (Mt 24: 14, 26:13, see also 13:38, 22:9, Lk 13:29)
    – relative to the training of His disciples
        (Mt 5:13 + 14, see also Mt 10:18, Lk 6:13, Mk 6:7, 11:17)
    – relative to the commissioning of His disciples
        (Mt 28: 18–20, Mk 16:15, Lk 24:46–49, Jn 20:21, Ac 1:8)

B. THE FOCUS OF DISCIPLING[21]

Discipling is at the heart of God's ordained strategy for world evangelism. (The
original Greek text of Mt 28:19 contains 'make disciples' as the sole imperative)
    – It secures both the quality and quantity of disciples intended by God
    – It secures in the disciple the proper motivation, message and method
    – It secures the extension of God's kingdom through explosive spiritual
      multiplication
    – It secures lasting spiritual fruit
    – It secures leadership for God's work

C. THE PURPOSE OF DISCIPLING

The twofold overall aim of all disciple-making:
– to develop Christians into mature, Christ-like disciples   (see Col 1:28)
– to develop Christians into reproducing multipliers   (see 2 Ti 2:2)

D. THE NATURE OF DISCIPLING

– A true disciple is a Christian who is totally committed to the Lord Jesus, desiring to learn from Him in order to become like Him
– For this learning process, the principle of imitation is absolutely fundamental
  – Jn 13:15, Mt 11:29; 1 Pe 2:21; 1 Jn 2:6
  – 1 Co 4:16, 11:1, Php 3:17, 1 Th 1:6, 2 Ti 1:13

E. THE PROTOTYPE OF DISCIPLING

– Jesus discipled through precept and example   (see 1 Jn 1:1)
– Jesus especially aimed at character development   (see Mk 10: 42–45)
– Jesus pursued spiritual multiplication   (see Jn 15:16, 17:20)
– Jesus trained His disciples in such a way that, simultaneously, He developed them as followers and as leaders   (see Mk 1:17)

F. THE KEY TO DISCIPLING

– In the disciple-making process, the Holy Spirit is the real agent; He enlightens the disciple, enables him to imitate, produces change and growth
– The disciple-maker merely functions as His instrument; he provides the environment for the Holy Spirit to accomplish His work
    Therefore, the discipler ought to be, in particular, a person of prayer and of the Word, and operating under the guidance and anointing of the Holy Spirit

G. THE SCOPE OF DISCIPLING

– individuals   (see 2 Ti 3:10–14, Ac 18:24–26)
– households   (see Ac 16:15 + 40, 20:20; Eph 6:4)
– groups   (see Mt 13:36–52, 17:19–21)
– congregations   (see Ac 11:26, Php 4:9, 2 Th 3:7–9)
– people groups ('nations')   (Mt 28:19, see also 25:31–33)

For further consideration:
    Keeping in mind that Jesus' lordship encompasses the mandate to be and make true disciples, how would you interpret Jn 15:8 and Isa 53:10 + 11?

27

Raising up Leaders

'... I will make you become fishers of men.'
(Mk 1:17)

A. THREE MAJOR STEPS IN DEVELOPING SPIRITUAL LEADERS

– selecting		(see Ac 16:1–3)
– training		
– informing :	through knowledge	(see 1 Ti 3:14)
– forming :	through insight and application	(see 1 Co 4:17)
– transforming :	through new values and priorities	(see 1 Ti 4:8; 2:1)
– releasing		(see 1 Co 16:10, 2 Ti 2:2)

B. DESIRABLE QUALITIES IN A PROSPECTIVE LEADER

– indispensable qualifications:
   Ac 6:3; 1 Pe 5:1–6; 1 Ti 3:2–13, Tit 1:5–9
– additional vital features:
   – a God-given vision   (see Pr 29:18, KJV)
   – a sanctified ambition to lead   (see 1 Ti 3:1)
– key questions to be considered when selecting:
   – can he follow?
   – can he be followed?
   – can he lead?

C. LESSONS FROM BARNABAS' TRAINING OF PAUL

– He took a risk in committing himself to Paul	(see Ac 9:26 + 27)
– He sought the optimal training environment for Paul	(see Ac 11:25 + 26)
– He enabled Paul to gather ministry experience	(see Ac 11:26,14:1 + 21–23)
– He made room for Paul to take initiative	(see Ac 13:9–11 + 16)
– He was willing to see Paul surpass him	(see Ac 13:2, 13:13 + 43)
– He gave Paul freedom to lead on his own	(see Ac 15:36–40)

D. LESSONS FROM PAUL'S TRAINING OF TIMOTHY

– He loved and appreciated Timothy	(2 Ti 1:2 + 4)
– He believed in Timothy's God-given potential	(see 1 Ti 4:12 + 14)
– He set an example for Timothy	(2 Ti 3:10 + 11 + 14)
– He instructed Timothy	(1 Ti 4:6–16)
– He challenged Timothy	(2 Ti 2:15, 4:1 + 2 + 5)
– He encouraged Timothy	(2 Ti 1:6 + 7)
– He delegated to Timothy	(1 Ti 1:3 + 4, 1 Th 3:2)
– He considered Timothy his equal	(Php 1:1, Ro 16:21)
– He committed himself to Timothy in prayer	(2 Ti 1:3)

E. CRUCIAL GUIDELINES FOR RAISING UP MULTIPLYING LEADERS

– Bathe the selection and training processes in prayer
– Target multiplication rather than mere addition
– Establish the proper example to be followed
– Apply apt coaching methods
– Provide on-the-job training
– Create room for the realization of all God-given potential
– Train leaders with the perspective that, hopefully, they may even surpass you
– Recognize that godly leaders cannot be mass-produced
– Bear in mind that not every potential trainee will actually possess the capacity and commitment needed to become a godly, effective and reproducing leader

F. GOOD LEADERSHIP COACHING NEVER GUARANTEES PERMANENT EXCELLENCE IN LEADERSHIP PERFORMANCE

– Men of the Bible whose training resulted in outstanding leadership:
   Joshua, Elisha, the eleven disciples, Paul, Timothy, Titus
– Men of the Bible whose leadership capacity declined:
   Saul, Joab, Solomon, Joash, Judas Iscariot, Demas

For further consideration:
   What would you name as the secret behind the amazing contrast between 1 Sa 22:2 and 1 Ch 11:10?

The ultimate example of leadership is Jesus. ...
The ultimate criterion is Christlike leadership.
JOHN HAGGAI (22)

It is not great talents God blesses so much
as great likeness to Jesus.
ROBERT MURRAY M'CHEYNE (23)

I.

SETTING AN EXAMPLE
TOWARDS
CHRIST-LIKENESS

28

Growing unto Maturity

'Whoever claims to live in him must walk as Jesus did.'
(1 Jn 2:6, NIV)

A. SPIRITUAL MATURITY EXPECTED

The New Testament standard for the Christian life is continual growth
   (1 Pe 2:2; 2 Pe 3:18; Ro 12:2; 2 Co 7:1)
The stage of spiritual childhood ought to be left behind
   (Eph 4:14, 1 Co 3:1, Heb 5: 12 + 13; see also 1 Jn 2:12–14)
The goal of all spiritual growth is maturity in Christ
   (Col 1:28, Eph 4:15; Heb 6:1; Php 3:14 + 15)

B. SPIRITUAL MATURITY CHARACTERIZED

The New Testament outlines maturity in Christ in various ways:
- following in Jesus' footsteps   (see 1 Pe 2:21)
- being conformed to Christ's image   (Ro 8:29)
- having grown up to Christ-likeness   (see 2 Co 3:18, 1 Jn 3:2)
- being like the Master   (see Lk 6:40, KJV)
- living in Christ's fullness   (see Eph 4:13, 3:19)
- being complete in Christ   (Col 1:28, NAS)

C. SPIRITUAL MATURITY HINDERED

According to Heb 5:11–14, symptoms of immaturity are:
- lacking spiritual alertness   (v. 11)
- lacking a deeper understanding of the Word   (v. 12)
- lacking skill in the use of the Word   (v. 13)
- lacking moral discernment   (v. 14)
Elements which stifle progress to maturity:
- slackness   (see Heb 6:11 + 12)
- neglect of the Word and of prayer   (see Col 3:16 and Jas 4:2)
- pride   (1 Pe 5:5, Pr 16:18)
- disobedience   (see Heb 4:6 + 11)
- unbelief   (see Heb 3:12 + 19, Ro 11:20)
- satanic opposition   (see Eph 6:11–13, Mt 13:19)

D. SPIRITUAL MATURITY FOSTERED

Elements which promote progress to maturity:
- a living relationship with Jesus Christ   (see Jn 15:4–7)
- the Holy Spirit's power at work   (see Eph 1:19, 3:20)
- God's grace   (see 2 Pe 1:3 + 4, Col 2:19)
- humility   (Jas 4:6)
- God's Word   (Ac 20:32, 2 Ti 3:16 + 17)
- prayer   (see Col 4:12, Php 1:9–11)
- faith   (Eph 6:16)
- suffering   (Ro 5:3 + 4, 1 Pe 1:6 + 7)

E. SPIRITUAL MATURITY EXHIBITED

A mature life will prove to be a fruitful life:
- in bringing forth the fruit of the Holy Spirit
- in attracting people to God
- in inspiring Christians to desire spiritual growth
- in discipling believers towards maturity and multiplication
- in making conquests for God through answered prayer
- in overcoming in times of temptation
- in defeating the purposes of Satan
- in glorifying God through life-style and service

For further consideration:
Study Simon Peter's spiritual progress: refer e.g. to Mt 14:28–31, 16:13–23, 26:31–35 + 69–75, Jn 18:10 + 11, 21:15–19, Ac 5:14–16 + 29, Gal 2:7–9, 2:11–14 and 1 Pe 3:8 + 9

29

Pursuing Excellence

'... He has done everything well ...'
(Mk 7:37, NIV)

A. SOME OF GOD'S EXCELLENCIES

– His character	(see Ps 8:9, KJV)
– His loving kindness	(Ps 36:7, KJV)
– His wisdom	(Isa 28:29)
– His will	(see Ro 12:2)
– His greatness	(Ps 150:2, KJV)
– His deeds	(Isa 12:5, NAS)

B. SOME CONTOURS OF SPIRITUAL EXCELLENCE

– the standard:	God	(see Mt 5:48)
– the model:	the Lord Jesus	(see Mt 17:5)
– the enabler:	the Holy Spirit	(see 2 Co 3:18)
– the goal:	Christ-likeness	(Ro 8:29)
– the purpose:	to reflect God's character	(see 1 Pe 1:15 + 16)
– the motive:	to please God	(see 1 Th 4:1)

C. SOME OBSERVATIONS REGARDING THE NATURE OF SPIRITUAL EXCELLENCE

- A real commitment to excellence will embrace all areas of life
- Spiritual excellence comprises pre-eminence in both what we *are* and what we *do*
- Spiritual excellence does not imply a state of perfection reached, but rather the process of its lifelong pursuit   (see Php 1:6)
- Spiritual excellence can never be achieved through self-effort, but only as we allow Christ to live His life through us   (see Heb 13:20 + 21)
- Spiritual excellence grows out of the commitment to become the best we can be with God's help
- God deserves our very best, in all respects, at all times
- A real commitment to spiritual excellence leaves no room for apathy, negligence and mediocrity

D. SOME PREREQUISITES FOR PROGRESSION IN THE PURSUIT OF SPIRITUAL EXCELLENCE

– direction	(see 1 Co 9:26)
– dedication	(see 1 Ti 2:4)
– determination	(see Php 3:12–15)
– diligence	(2 Co 8:7, KJV)
– discipline	(see 1 Co 9:25)
– dependence on God's grace	(see 2 Pe 1:3 + 4)

E. SOME MAJOR AREAS CHRISTIANS OUGHT TO EXCEL IN

– love	(see 2 Co 8:7)	– work	(see Col 3:23)
– faith	(see 2 Co 8:7)	– ministry	(see 2 Co 6:3–10)
– relationships	(see Ro 12:9–21)	– speech	(see Col 4:6)
– thought life	(see Php 4:8)	– appearance	(see 1 Co 6:19 + 20)
– conduct	(see Php 1:10)	– good deeds	(see Tit 3:8)

F. SOME QUESTIONS HELPFUL TO TEST THE EXCELLENCE OF ACTIONS

– Is this according to God's will?
– is this pleasing in God's sight?
– Is this glorifying God?
– Is this worthy of God?
– Is this a responsible use of God-given talents?

G. SOME BIBLICAL EXAMPLES OF SPIRITUAL EXCELLENCE

ex. Joseph	(Ge 41:38 + 39)	ex. Josiah	(2 Ki 23:25)
ex. Moses	(Nu 12:3)	ex. Job	(Job 1:8)
ex. Hezekiah	(2 Ki 18:5)	ex. Daniel	(Da 5:12 + 14)
ex. Jesus:			

> e.g. His love for God, faith, prayerfulness, obedience, humility;
> His love for people, compassion, servanthood, forgiveness

For further consideration:
In the light of Lk 6:40 (NAS) and 1 Pe 5:2 + 3, what parts can discipleship and leadership training play in developing a spirit of excellence?

30

Refining through Fire

'Although he was a Son, he learned obedience
through what he suffered ...'
(Heb 5:8)

A. REFINING – A FAMILIAR IMAGE IN GOD'S WORD

– God is the refiner	(Zec 13:9, Isa 48:10)
– God refines to test	(Jer 9:7, 1 Pe 1:6 + 7)
– God refines to purify	(see Mal 3:3, Ps 66:10)
– God's refining may be in vain	(see Jer 6:28–30)

B. REASONS WHY GOD TAKES US THROUGH CHARACTER REFINEMENT PROCESSES

– to increase our dependence on Him	(see 2 Co 1:8–10, 12:9 + 10)
– to adjust us more to His will	(1 Pe 4:1 + 2, see also Php 2:13)
– to produce holiness in us	(Heb 12:10 + 11, see also Jn 17:14–17)
– to lead us towards spiritual maturity	(Jas 1:2–4, see also Mt 5:43–48)
– to teach us humility	(see Dt 8:2 + 16)
– to teach us endurance	(Ro 5:3, Jas 1:2 + 3)
– to teach us contentment	(see Php 4:11–13, 2 Co 12:10)
– to share His Father's love with us	(see Heb 12:5–8, Rev 3:19)
– to bless us	(1 Pe 3:14, 4:14, Dt 8:16)
– to prepare us for eternity	(2 Co 4:17, Ro 8:17 + 18)
– to enable us to help others	(2 Co 1:3–5, see also Heb 2:17 + 18)

C. BIBLE FIGURES WHO WENT THROUGH A REFINING PROCESS

ex. Joseph	(see Ge 37:5–9 + 28, 39:20, 42:6 + 9)
ex. Moses	(see Ex 2:11 + 12, 3:11)
ex. Hannah	(see 1 Sa 1:1–11, 1:27–2:1)
ex. Job	(see Job 42:1–6)
ex. Nebuchadnezzar	(see Da 4:29–37)
ex. Paul	(see 2 Co 12:5–10)

D. VARIOUS REFINING MEASURES GOD MAY UTILIZE AS INDICATED BY SCRIPTURE

- trials, temptations, tribulations, distress; discipline
- persecution, imprisonment, captivity, exile; poverty
- diseases, epidemics; bad harvests, drought, famine; oppression, war
- delayed answers to prayers

E. POSSIBLE WRONG RESPONSES TO GOD'S DEALINGS

- discouragement   (Heb 12:15)
- fear   (see Ps 27:1–3, Php 1:28)
- unbelief   (Heb 10:35)
- bitterness   (see Heb 12:15)
- resignation   (see Heb 10:38 + 39, 12:3)

F. RIGHT RESPONSES TO GOD'S REFINING MEASURES

- seeking God   (Jas 5:13, see also Ps 78:34)
- considering God at work   (see Ge 50:20, Job 19:21)
- trusting God   (1 Pe 4:19, see also Job 13:15, KJV)
- giving thanks   (1 Th 5:18, Php 4:6)
- expecting blessing   (Mt 5:10–12)

G. CORNERSTONES OF FAITH IN THE FACE OF ADVERSITY

- Nothing can separate us from God's love   (Ro 8:35–39)
- Nobody can take us out of His hand   (Jn 10:28–30)
- Jesus has overcome the world   (Jn 16:33)
- Our faith overcomes the world   (1 Jn 5:4)

For further consideration:
   In view of the fact that Saul was persecuting David, what does the latter's attitude in 1 Sa 24:1–20 and 26:1–25 reveal about his character?

31

Going for Heavenly Treasures

'looking to Jesus ... who for the joy that was set before him
endured the cross, despising the shame ...'
(Heb 12:2)

A. GOD'S WORD EXHORTS US TO HAVE A HEAVENLY PERSPECTIVE

- Mt 6:19–21, 6:24–33, Jn 6:27; Lk 9:25; Mt 10:28; Mk 10:23; Lk 12:15–21
- 1 Ti 6:6–19
- 1 Pe 2:11 + 12, 2 Pe 3:10–14
- 1 Jn 2:15–17
- Jas 4:13–16, 5:1–8

B. MEN WHO FAILED BECAUSE OF AN EARTHLY PERSPECTIVE

ex. Gideon	(Jdg 8:24–27)
ex. Solomon	(1 Ki 11:1–11)
ex. Judas	(Mt 26:14–16., Jn 12:6)
ex. Ananias	(Ac 5:1–6)
ex. Demas	(2 Ti 4:10)

C. TESTING WHERE WE STAND

- What do I take most pleasure in?
- What am I most concerned about?
- What am I most committed to?
- What do I put most trust in?

D. MEN WHO PURSUED A HEAVENLY PERSPECTIVE

ex. Abraham	(Heb 11:9 + 10)
ex. Jacob	(see Ge 47:9)
ex. David	(1 Ch 29:15)

ex. Jesus   (see Mt 6:10, Jn 9:4 + 5)
ex. Paul   (see 2 Co 4:17–5:10)

E. TRAITS OF A HEAVENLY PERSPECTIVE

– a desire to grow in the knowledge of Jesus Christ (see Php 3:8–10)
– a desire to live for the glory of God   (see Eph 1:5 + 6 + 12)
– a desire to pursue the things of the Holy Spirit   (see Ro 8:5)
– a desire to progress in godliness   (see 1 Ti 4:7 + 8)
– a desire to prove a faithful servant   (see Mt 25:19–23)
– a desire to hasten Christ's return   (see 2 Pe 3:12)

F. ESSENTIAL: A PILGRIM'S MENTALITY

– he is on his way to his real and better home   (see Jn 14:2 + 3, Heb 11:13–16)
– he lays aside every hindrance along his way   (see Heb 12:1, 1 Co 9:24 + 25)
– he focuses on eternal values   (see 2 Co 4:18, Col 3:1 + 2)
– he seeks to prepare for heaven   (see 1 Pe 2:11, 1 Jn 3:2 + 3)
– he endures suffering in view of eternal glory   (see 2 Co 4:17, Ro 8:18)
– he looks forward to a heavenly inheritance   (see 1 Pe 1:4, Heb 9:15)
– he expects to reign with Christ   (see 2 Ti 2:12, Rev 5:10)

G. WAYS OF LAYING UP TREASURES IN HEAVEN

– through living totally under Christ's lordship   (see Mk 10:29 + 30)
– through developing a righteous character   (see Pr 10:25)
– through labouring for God   (see 1 Co 15:58)
– through soul-winning   (see Da 12:3)
– through a prayer inheritance amongst the nations   (see Ps 2:8)
– through acts of kindness to other people   (see Mt 25: 31–46, 19:21)

For further consideration:
   Compare the responses described in 2 Ki 5:15 + 16 with 2 Ki 5:19–27.

Leadership is an awesome responsibility ... God wants you to develop the potential He has given you. The extent to which your performance fails to live up to your potential is the extent to which you are failing God. The extent to which you are fulfilling your potential is the extent to which you are serving God.

JOHN HAGGAI (24)

Notes

1 P.T. Chandapilla, *The Master-Trainer* (Gospel Literature Service, Bombay; 1974), p. x

2 David L. Hocking, *Be A Leader People Follow* (Regal Books, Ventura, California; 1979), p. 17

3 Ted W. Engstrom, *The Making of a Christian Leader* (Pyrenee Books, Grand Rapids, Michigan; 1976), p. 39

4 Chua Wee Hian, *Learning to lead* (IVP, Leicester; 1987), p. 55

5 The abbreviation ex. is used for 'see the example of'

6 Derek Prime, *Christian Leadership* (Pickering & Inglis, London; 1964/1980), p. 55

7 D.E. Hoste, in: Dr. & Mrs. Howard Taylor, *Hudson Taylor in Early Years. The Growth Of A Soul* (CIM, London; 1911), p. xvii

8 J. Oswald Sanders, *Spiritual Leadership* (Lakeland, London; 1967/1981), p. 70

9 Stephen F. Olford, 'The Power of Preaching' *Christianity Today* (December 7, 1979), p. 1617

10 Sanders, op cit, p. 75

11 Charles Sibthorpe, *A Man under Authority* (Kingsway Publications, Eastbourne; 1984), p. 168

12 Sanders, op cit, p. 44

13 John Haggai, *Lead On!* (Word Publishing, Milton Keynes; 1986),
    p. 81

14 Andrew Murray, *How To Raise Your Children For Christ* (Bethany
    Fellowship, Minneapolis, Minnesota; 1975), p. 23

15 J. Hudson Taylor, in: Marshall Broomhall (Ed.) *Hudson Taylor's
    Legacy* (Hodder and Stoughton, London; 1974) p. 31

16 Ralph Mahoney, *The Making of a Leader* (World Missionary
    Assistance Plan, Burbank, California; 1985), p. 204

17 Hocking, op cit, p. 141

18 Carl Wilson, *With Christ In The School Of Disciple Building. A Study
    of Christ's Method Of Building Disciples* (Zondervan, Grand Rapids,
    Michigan; 1976), p. 52

19 Myron Rush, *The New Leader. A Revolutionary Approach to Effective
    Leadership* (Victor Books, Wheaton, Illinois; 1987), p. 57

20 Leroy Eims, *Be the Leader You Were Meant to Be. What the Bible Says
    about Leadership* (Victor Books, Wheaton, Illinois; 1975) p. 79

21 For more detailed information on the Biblical foundation and
    practice of discipleship training, see the author's book *Following
    Jesus. A Handbook On Basic Discipleship For Individual And Group
    Study* (Hodder and Stoughton, London; 1987)

22 Haggai, op cit, pp. xii and 6

23 Robert Murray M'Cheyne, in: Hian, op cit, p. 100

24 Haggai, op cit, p. xii7